ADVANCED EMAIL MARKETING

All organization and personal names in this book are intended to be fictional, and any similarities to actual entities or individuals are coincidental. Designations used by companies to distinguish their products are often claimed as trademarks or registered trademarks. In all instances in which Lyris Technologies is aware of a claim, the product or brand names appear in initial capital or all capital letters. Readers, however, should contact the appropriate companies for more complete information regarding trademarks and registration.

Lyris Technologies, Inc.
5858 Horton St., Suite 270
Emeryville, CA 94608
www.lyris.com
(800) 768-2929
(510) 844-1600
emailbook@lyris.com

Art Direction and Design: Frances Baca Design
Technical Illustration: Judith Ogus

ISBN: 0-9744393-0-4

ADVANCED EMAIL MARKETING

Using Email to Achieve Sales and Marketing Goals

JIM STERNE

About *Advanced Email Marketing*

THE AUTHOR

Jim Sterne produced the world's first "Marketing on the Internet" seminar series in 1994. Today, Sterne is an internationally known speaker on electronic marketing and customer interaction, and a consultant to Fortune 500 companies and Internet entrepreneurs. He focuses his twenty years in sales and marketing on measuring the value of a Web site as a medium for creating and strengthening customer relationships.

Sterne has written five books, including:

- *Web Metrics: Proven Methods for Measuring Web Site Success,* John Wiley & Sons, 2002

- *World Wide Web Marketing,* 3rd Edition, John Wiley & Sons, 2001

- *E-Mail Marketing*, John Wiley & Sons, 2000

- *Customer Service on the Internet,* 2nd Edition, John Wiley & Sons, 2000

- *What Makes People Click: Advertising on the Web,* Que, 1997

In 2002, Sterne founded Emetrics.org, focused on Web analytics, Web metrics, and Web site analysis. His company, Target Marketing (www.targeting.com), is dedicated to helping companies understand the possibilities and manage the realities of conducting business online.

THE PUBLISHER

Lyris Technologies develops the world's best-selling software and services for email marketing and publishing. Lyris has built its email expertise since starting in 1994; at the time of publication, more than 4,000 businesses worldwide use its solutions. Additional information is available at www.lyris.com.

Contents

Introduction

This book is for the professional email marketer who wants to take control, own the email marketing process, and objectively and systematically measure results.

This book is *not* intended to celebrate the virtues of email marketing, nor condemn the scourge that is unsolicited commercial email. You already know that email is fast, inexpensive, superb at relationship building, and a great way to ruin a reputation if you send out anything that smacks of spam. We hold those truths to be self-evident, and move forward in an effort to determine just *how* powerful, fast, inexpensive, and superb email marketing can be.

HOW TO USE THIS BOOK

Advanced Email Marketing covers a broad range of email marketing topics through instructional text, real-world examples, and hands-on worksheets. Each chapter has four different components, intended to be read either together or individually.

Key Concepts

The beginning of each chapter introduces selected issues and questions that most marketers and their organizations face in the course of creating, maintaining, or improving an email marketing operation. I address these topics broadly, explaining why they're important and providing relevant background information.

The Story: Acme Bike Corporation

At the core of *Advanced Email Marketing* is a work of fiction—a narrative about a fictional business and its team's efforts to use email to assess and improve a number of sales and marketing processes. In this part of each chapter, I illustrate the Key Concepts with examples that may reflect your own experiences, or those you'll probably have when you ramp up your company's email marketing program. You can read more about the Acme Bike Corp. and our protagonist, Ed the Email Marketer, in the next section.

Summary

This brief section of bullet points lists the major concepts presented in the chapter. It's meant as both a wrap-up and as a quick guide for your future reference.

Worksheet

At the end of each chapter, you'll find a set of worksheet questions and matrices that ask you to apply the chapter's concepts to *your* business. I encourage you to complete these exercises—your take-away from the book will be far more permanent that way, and you'll likely find it easier to initiate new steps in your organization almost immediately.

MORE ABOUT THE STORY

Many books include case studies or other real-world examples to educate their readers. In *Advanced Email Marketing* I've chosen to use a single organization—the Acme Bike Corporation—to this end. You'll not only see how an email marketing concept is applied to a particular circumstance, but also how the various concepts build upon one another.

Our story concerns Acme Bikes, a fictional medium-sized company that sells bicycles and bicycle parts. Some of its products are inexpensive and mass-produced, while others are hand-crafted and quite pricey. As you'd imagine, Acme sells through several different channels: mass market chain stores; independent, specialty retailers; and online, via its website. The company also has a series of Acme-branded service departments within the stores of its larger retail partners, and a team of bicycle mechanics to staff them. All in all, it's a mixed bag with a lot of different customer segments to please.

The central character of our story is named Ed. Ed the Email Marketer—Everymarketer Ed, if you will—is a marketing professional who believes in deliberate, continuous improvement rather than random attempts and uncalculated results. Ed has learned by reading books, by considering the successes and failures of others, and by running some of his own campaigns. He especially likes a comment made by direct marketing expert Herschel Gordon Lewis:

> "Moving 'Click here' up (higher) in email always helps response.
> Why?
> Three words: I don't care."

Does HTML email always pull better than straight text? Is it always more effective to send newsletters on Thursday afternoons instead of Monday mornings? Should the offer always be in the subject line? Ed knows a litany of email marketing success rules, but he also knows that his mileage *will* vary.

Ed now has the chance to put his knowledge to work as a new hire at Acme Bikes. This is his opportunity to discretely measure what works best in specific situations, to get his arms around testing…

> Testing the format of an email newsletter
> Testing the value of an email offer
> Testing the profitability of an advertising campaign
> Testing the patience of his colleagues

In an ideal world, you would capture all of the information necessary to track the value of the work you do. You would measure every variation in your marketing messages and methods to determine the optimal approach to every marketing move. In an ideal world, you would be in control of all aspects of your email marketing program, and all improvements to lead generation and sales could easily be attributed to your skills and talents. In an ideal world, you'd have the budget you need to do the job right. And in an ideal world, everybody you work with would understand what you were trying to accomplish and would help you get there.

Ed doesn't live in that world, however—none of us do.

In the subsequent chapters, you'll follow Ed through numerous challenges. The scenarios cover critical topics such as goal setting, campaign testing, measurement and analysis, and, ultimately, "closing the loop" from marketing to sales. Overarching all of these issues and examples is a strong emphasis on integration—for example, integrating:

- the various marketing components of email, advertising, and public relations;

- the technology driving email, the web, and CRM systems; and

- the different stakeholders in a business organization.

Complete this book—including the Worksheets at the end of each chapter—and you'll be a big step closer to owning *your* email marketing process, as Ed does his.

CHAPTER 1

Email in the Organizational Food Chain

KEY CONCEPTS

Email competes for resources. Email marketing may be top of mind for you, given your chosen profession or current focus, but in most organizations it's one component of many competing for limited resources.

Email isn't always well understood. While email marketing is sexy enough these days to be highly *valued* by many different people in an organization, it's also new enough to be widely *misunderstood*. Various stakeholders may know that it's "important"—but they may not know what that really means. An initial challenge for the email marketer, then, is to understand how email fits into the organization's current marketing mix, sales process, and business culture, and manage expectations accordingly.

THE STORY

ED ARRIVED AT THE ACME BIKE CORPORATION bright and early on Monday morning, eager to start his new position. The first person he saw was Victoria, the VP of Sales and Marketing. "Morning, Ed. Glad you could join us. You're right on time to meet the troops. Come with me," and she was out the door.

Ed followed Victoria, his boss' boss, to the conference room. Ed was to report to Mark, the Director of Marketing, who along with Ava, the Director of Advertising, reported to Victoria. Ed had met all three of them during the interview process. But this was the first time he had met Derek, who said he was responsible for direct mail promotions. *(Figure 1.1, p.14)*

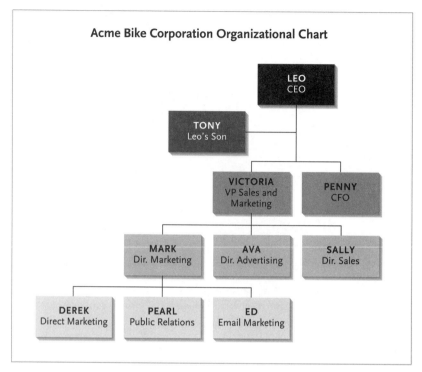

FIGURE 1.1

"Here's the game plan, people," Victoria started while Ed and Derek were still shaking hands and the others had not yet settled into their seats. "We've got three initiatives that need our attention, and they all need to be big wins. Now that the Interbike trade show is behind us, I need you to focus, plan, and execute. Jobs are literally at stake."

Ed saw Derek and Ava glance over at Mark.

"First," Victoria carried on, "we're gearing up to launch our new high-end bike, the 'Gold Standard.' Ava and Mark, you need to work out messaging that will put a smile on Leo's face. I want a roll-out game plan outlined by the end of the month for that message and delivering it, but first we've got to get Leo to sign off on it.

"Next, sales at our Acme brand service departments have hit an even lower low, and we need to bump up their numbers this quarter or Leo's going to pull the plug on them. And if *that* happens, Pearl will have her hands full with the press to spin it positively. I want some really sharp ideas—I want to be amazed at the ways you can get people into service departments."

The quick smiles around the table proved the team was listening—but Victoria didn't stop for a breather. Ever.

"Third up: sales of our low-end 'Silver Dollar' bike. They're going OK, but if you're going to get bonuses this year, they're going to have to ramp up a lot steeper. Fortunately, we have Ed here, who's going to implement an email marketing program to promote online sales. Right, Ed?"

Ed opened his mouth to say he had several ideas already, but he never got the chance.

"I'm sure you will. Mark, I want you in my office with last quarter's research results. Ava, Leo's agreed to keep the advertising budget where it is for the moment, but you should have an idea or two for trimming if the time comes. Derek, I know your hands are tied until we get the messaging together, so I want you to work with Ed on integrating online and offline promotions. And Ed, any questions?"

Victoria's rapidfire approach was a bit disconcerting. But it was Ed's first day and there was no time like the present to remind Victoria that he wouldn't be productive until he got the lay of the land.

"To start with," Ed answered. "Who's Leo?"

"Leo Acme, the head of this organization. He's got a gift for the marketplace, so we listen when he growls and shakes his mane. We make a lot of decisions and do all the work, but Leo likes to keep his hand in almost everything and he's been right on the mark for decades. He's very particular about messaging and knows what he likes. Ava, I want six messaging ideas on my desk by Wednesday noon. Mark, six more from you. Any other questions?"

Ed saw that leadership-by-steamroller seemed to be Victoria's style, so he merely watched the others as they nodded their heads with knowing looks.

"Good," Victoria wrapped up. "In that case, Mark, show Ed to his desk and have him show you how he's going to save the day."

With that, Victoria was gone. Ed pondered his choice of new company. Derek disappeared. Ava looked intently into her PDA. Mark grinned. "Welcome to Victoria's Mad House," he said to Ed.

SUMMARY

- In any group, it's clearly important to figure out the responsibilities and motivations of your teammates. Especially those who may not recognize that *they're* on the team, too!

- Email marketing may be the exciting newcomer these days, but by no means does it stand alone. Many other mediums compete for budget and attention.

- Expectations for email marketing's potential may be all over the map. Make sure you know what your colleagues expect, and manage those expectations accordingly.

WORKSHEET

- Which departments or individuals are *directly* involved in your organization's email marketing operation? How can they influence it?

- Which departments or individuals are *indirectly* involved in your organization's email marketing operation? How can they influence it?

- Are the key stakeholders above positively or negatively inclined— or indifferent—towards email marketing?

- Do the key stakeholders above understand "email marketing" in more or less the same way you do? If there's a gap, what steps can you take to close it?

CHAPTER 2

Setting and Aligning Goals

KEY CONCEPTS

Goals and measurement go hand-in-hand. As the Cheshire Cat said, if you don't know where you are going, then any road will take you there. The sentiment is highly applicable to your business; in fact, we can express it as a neat circular argument:

Without clear goals, there's no need to measure anything; without measuring, there's no way to know if the work you're doing is helping to achieve your goals.

So, you need to set goals. Doing so enables you to identify the specific measurements that verify your progress. Sales may be your end game, but tracking the number and type of people who subscribe to your newsletter, visit your Web site, enter your contests, or submit their personal information will tell you if you're moving towards or away from your goals.

Goal alignment throughout the organization is key. Along the way, you have to spend time monitoring departmental and individual goals to make sure that all are properly aligned with the organization's overall goals. Any disconnects that arise will likely throw some part of the business off-course, jeopardizing your chances of success.

And that's especially the case for marketing, where critical eyes and budgets cuts are the norm these days. Goals or milestones are the stepping stones to making money, and the marketer who can demonstrate clear success in helping to achieve them is likely to be well rewarded.

THE STORY

AFTER THE TEAM MEETING ENDED, Ed sat down with Mark, the Director of Marketing and Ed's direct supervisor. Ed was determined to cut through the morning's turmoil and find out what Acme Bikes was trying to accomplish. He knew that everything started with vision and depended on turning that vision into specific, measurable goals. He asked Mark to give him a rundown of the company's objectives.

"At the end of the day, it's all about increasing sales. Victoria's comments about jobs being at stake and departments closing weren't just for show. We really do need to kick up the sales figures around here. For some people at Acme Bikes, that means putting more account reps on the road, visiting dealers. For some, it's mailing more coupons. And for others, it's improving customer service. But all of it revolves around finding, wooing, closing, and retaining customers: building customer relationships. Like road signs that indicate how far it is to the next town, there are innumerable milestones that tell us if we're headed in the right direction away from obscurity and toward greater profitability."

Ed assured his new boss that he was preaching to the choir. Ed was a numbers man first, and a creative type second.

"Good," Mark replied. 'Then you and I will be able to accomplish something that others around here have shied away from: manage by measurement! Make sure you really understand our goals, because then you can make things happen without having to get a committee together to argue about it."

Ed reached into a file folder, and pulled out a typewritten sheet. "Here's a list of goals we considered at my last job—we didn't aim for all of them, of course, but they were helpful for brainstorming and discussions." (*Table 2.1, p.19*)

THREE DAYS LATER, Victoria stopped by Ed's desk. She was still considering the twelve sample marketing messages the team had created, trying to guess which would resonate best with Acme's CEO, Leo. She dropped the list on Ed's desk. "Which one?"

Ed decided to deal with Victoria as straight as possible. "Not my department—I'm not a creative expert. But once you narrow it down to three, I'll tell you which one will work best. In fact, I can prove it."

"You can prove it." Victoria looked skeptical to the point of disbelief.

"The miracle of email marketing," Ed smiled confidently.

"Why not prove the best of twelve?"

	Financial Goals	Non-Financial Goals
Sales	• Close X total accounts/deals/transactions • Close Y new accounts/deals/transactions • Close Z repeat accounts/deals/transactions • Increase closure rate by X% • Increase add-on/support sales by $X or Y% • Hit $X total business • Increase total business by Y% • Increase business for product X by Y% • Increase margin by X% • Increase travel budget ROI by X% • Increase trade show ROI by X%	• Increase the number of repeat customers by X • Decrease the sales cycle length by X • Decrease shopping cart abandons by X • Increase the # of lead referrals per month • Increase # of highly satisfied customers • Increase # of customers who buy more than once • Decrease # of irate customers
Marketing	• Generate $X in sales from campaign Y • Increase campaign ROI by X% • Reduce marketing costs by X%	• Generate X new leads/opportunities • Increase new leads/opportunities by Y% • Increase new subscribers by X% or Y • Increase new subscriptions from Domain X • Reduce unsubscribes by X% or Y • Reduce spam complaints by X% • Increase confirmation rates by X% or Y • Increase brand/product exposure by X% • Increase press mentions by X% • Increase testimonials by X% • Increase clickthroughs by X% • Increase visits to Page X by Y% • Increase duration of session visit by X% • Increase the number of members at Interest Stage X • Increase the rate at which members reach Interest Stage X

TABLE 2.1

"Too many variables. If I add in a few other factors, like different lists, the test will become unmanageable. Testing three creative messages is a good starting point."

"How soon can you 'prove it'?" Victoria replied, with a distinct challenge in her voice.

"How about...three days?"

"HOW ARE YOU GOING to deliver in three days?" Ava asked Ed, looking worried.

Derek was bewildered. Mark was decidedly unhappy. "Well?" Mark asked.

Mark had called them into the conference room after Victoria told him that *she* would be picking Ed's replacement. Somebody a bit more "realistic."

"Our house list has email addresses for 100,000 consumers, right?" countered Ed.

"Yeah."

"Give me the three messages and I'll turn them around in three days."

"And you're going to be able to prove to Leo which one he's going to like best?"

"No, I'll be able to prove to Leo which will sell more bicycles."

Ava rolled her eyes. Mark and Derek looked at each other.

"He wants to sell bikes, right?"

Mark gave Ed the message copy. Derek gave Ed four days before Acme Bikes would be recruiting a new email marketing manager.

SUMMARY

- Make sure that your department or personal objectives are consistent with the organization's overall goals. And if you don't know what your organization is trying to achieve, ask!

- Break your goals down into clearly identified specifics. "Generating more revenue" is a fine overall objective and it's certainly measurable; to be useful at the day-to-day level, however, broad goals need to be distilled into project-size pieces.

- Pursue your goals with marketing projects that are themselves clearly defined, for example, a test campaign with a manageable number of variables. Email analytics will then be an effective tool for *proving* the best approach to a particular problem or opportunity.

WORKSHEET

- How up-to-date are you about your organization's goals? Complete the table below to assess your awareness, and to see if your company, department, and individual goals are properly aligned.

Company Goal	Department/Division Goal	Individual Goal
Increase revenue 10%	*Increase monthly conversion rate*	*Close five more pending sales*

- Do you have clear criteria for measuring the progress and completion of your goals? Fill out the following table to gauge if you're moving in the right direction.

Goal	Success Measurement	Priority	Target Date
Increase monthly conversion rate	*At least three extra deals per rep*	*1*	*Month-end*

- If it's difficult to articulate success metrics for your objectives, what information or tools do you need? Do other key stakeholders in your organization need to be involved in this process?

CHAPTER 3 The Medium
Helps Determine
the Message

KEY CONCEPTS

Messages must resonate with your customers. Perhaps the most difficult lesson to learn about marketing, whether you are a company founder, an advertising copywriter, a product manager, or a Web designer, is that your central theme, your basic brand message, should not be what you think sounds best or looks great on a billboard; rather, it should be that which speaks to the hearts and minds of your prospective customers. Your message should not be about *you,* but about *them.*

Email is an effective message-testing tool. While you have likely used email to drive Web traffic and sales, you may not have used it as a tool for testing your brand message. Due to its inherent measurability, email is well-suited to this task. All that remains is determining which message resonates best and distilling it into the fewest, most transferable words possible.

THE STORY

CEO LEO'S OFFICE WAS LARGE enough to have its own conference table, and he sat Ed down right next to him.

"First of all son, I just wancha to understand that I got neckties older than you, OK? My daddy founded this company, and I've run it up from his retail store in Raleigh to the manufacturing marvel it is today. I've done it by the skin of my teeth and the sweat of my brow. But much more than that, I've done it by knowing what fires folks up about bikes. Do you like bikes, Ed?"

"Well, yes, I..."

"Because I really *love* bicycles, son, and I'm going to tell you what. I've got three advertising choices in front of me, and the one that says 'Acme Bikes Are Best' floats my boat. It says what it means, and it means what it says, and I *like* it. It rings true. Now, Victoria here tells me that you don't agree with me. Is that right?"

"Well...sir...It's not that I disagree..."

"Good. Then it's settled. I want to see 'Acme Bikes Are Best' on everything. Right, son?"

Ed decided it was no longer a matter of being the new kid on the block. If he was going to have to put up with Victoria's mayhem and Leo's growling, then it just wasn't a job worth having. He might as well go out with his integrity intact.

"Bad idea, Leo," he said.

Pins could have dropped. Jaws did.

"Beg pardon?" Leo sounded like he'd smoked cigars for the better part of twenty years.

"Bad idea," Ed said again.

Leo winced. Then he scowled. "Neckties..."

"You see, Leo, in our tests, 'Acme Bikes Are Best' definitely got more people to come to our Web site than the other two, but..."

"Victoria, the only question left is whether this inconsiderate young fool is hard of hearing or just a simpleton."

Victoria turned to Mark, who was looking down at his hands. Ed went right ahead.

"But," Ed said, "they weren't the people we wanted. They weren't the people *you* wanted. That phrase brought in the wrong people."

"Mark, what the heck is he talking about? Who are the wrong people?"

"He, uh...I..." Mark sputtered.

"The answer to your first question, Leo," Ed went on, "is that I *am* a simpleton. I look at simple numbers and they tell a simple story. Let me show you and answer your second question." Time to go for broke, Ed thought. This should be fun.

"This report tells the whole story," Ed said, laying down a color bar chart in front of Leo and sliding three more copies down the table to the others. *(Figure 3.1, p.25)*

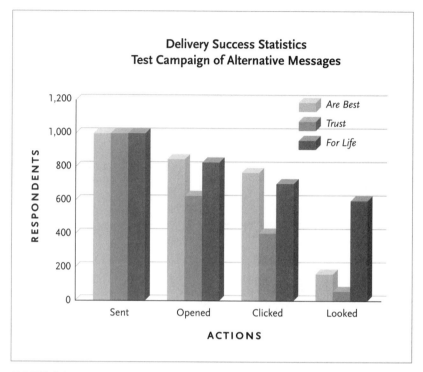

Delivery Success Statistics
Test Campaign of Alternative Messages

FIGURE 3.1

"We did a test campaign of a thousand emails to three different groups in our consumer database. Each group was the same—that is, randomly selected—except for getting a different marketing message. The 'Bikes Are Best' message was opened more than the other two, and it got more people to click through from the email to our Web site than the other two. But that's not the metric that matters."

Leo was squinting at the report with his lips tight.

Ed went on, "'Trust Acme Bikes' scored the worst in every category, so we can drop that. But look what happens on the right—'Acme Bikes For Life' scored four times higher than 'Are Best' at getting people to look at more than three pages on our Web site. Most of the 'Are Best' recipients just clicked through to the landing page and left. They didn't look at anything beyond that—they were the wrong people."

Victoria, Mark, and Ava glanced back and forth between the chart and the head of the table.

"The wrong people," Leo said. "Just because they didn't look at more than one page of our Web site?"

"Well," said Ed. "It goes a little deeper than that. I asked Ava to help me out testing the brand impact."

"The brand impact?" Leo said.

Ava handed out a single sheet to the other four at the table. (*Figure 3.2*)

A **brand impression** is the opinion about your company formed when people:

- See an ad
- Visit the Web site
- Call and talk to the receptionist
- Are put on hold and hear "Your call is important to us"
- Walk into a store
- Read the newspaper ad
- Talk to a sales rep
- Wait for and read product literature
- Talk to colleagues about you
- Read about the firm in the financial pages
- Read product reviews
- Make a purchase
- Try to use the product
- Call customer service
- Talk to friends about their experience

A brand impression is the sum total of an individual's feelings and the aggregate of those feelings across a whole marketplace.

FIGURE 3.2

"Usually," Ava said after everybody had a chance to scan the page, "you find out how people feel by asking them. You walk up to them on the street with a clipboard, or call them on the phone, or ask a research company to run a focus group. All of that takes a lot of time, so in the three days we had, we did a combination of email questionnaires and pop-up surveys on our Web site.

"To measure the impact of online advertising on our brand, I used four metrics that a marketing research company recommends:[1]

---

1. Metrics recommended by Dynamic Logic (www.dynamiclogic.com).

Awareness: Do they recognize the name of the company and product?

Message Association: Do they connect our slogan with our company and product?

Purchase Intent: Are they more likely to buy after hearing our slogan?

Brand Favorability: Do they feel better about our company after hearing the slogan?

"The surveys delivered somewhat soft answers, but 'For Life' scored 20% higher than 'Are Best' across all four categories, and 60% higher than "Trust Acme Bikes.'"

"So regardless of what I like," said Ed, "I believe 'Acme Bikes For Life' would be the most successful slogan."

Leo looked at the reports. He looked at Ava. He frowned at Mark. He glowered at Victoria. Then he glared at Ed. " OK, that's it then. 'Acme Bikes For Life' is the banner we fly. Any questions?" Heads were shaking.

"Just one," said Ed, enjoying the moment and pushing his luck. Leo's eyes narrowed. "How much do the revenues of our Acme brand service departments have to increase in order to keep them open?"

Leo's expression didn't change. "I want an increase of four percent in net profit by the quarter's end."

"Can you tell me which services are the most profitable and which are the least?"

"Talk to Penny. This meeting is over."

SUMMARY

- Email analytics can be a useful tool even when applied to measuring "soft" issues such as branding.

- Identify the metrics you would use to determine whether one message or another resonates best with your audience—for example, the number of pages viewed, the duration of a site visit, the number of contact forms submitted, etc.

- Consider launching an internal marketing campaign to explain the concept of branding and how it is affected by everything the company does—not only by what goes on in the advertising department.

WORKSHEET

- What brand promises are you making to your customers? What feedback do you get from customers regarding your success in delivering on your promises? Who is responsible for monitoring—and then acting on—this feedback?

- In what ways have you used email to communicate your brand message(s)? How could you use email to test the effectiveness of different messages?

- What metrics could you use to determine which marketing messages resonate best with your prospects and customers?

- Complete the following table with the results of your latest campaign. How does the feedback you received from the email marketing component correlate with that from the other media?

Brand Message	Owner or Champion	Interview or Focus Group Results	Survey Results	Email Test Results	Overall Rank Among All Test Messages
"Acme Bikes for Life"	Derek— Direct Mail	n/a	20% better response than second-place	Best click-through results	1

4 Driving Traffic—
Online and Off

KEY CONCEPTS

Offline sales—and measurement—are still important. Not every company sells everything online. Most of us are trying to figure out how to use our Web sites to influence offline behavior as well. We're trying to get people to call for an appointment, agree to see a sales rep, or get in their car, drive down to the mall, walk into a shop, and buy our product.

When broadcast advertising isn't focused on brand-building, it does its best to get people to, "Call now," because, "Operators are standing by." If you sell products via direct TV (a.k.a. infomercials), you know precisely how many calls your promotion generates and at exactly which minute into the broadcast people call.

Email can illuminate the connection between HQ and Retail. Print ads and direct mail have often been the bridge between the marketing office and the retail store through the use of coupons. Email can play the very same role. Clickthroughs and phone calls tell a detailed story about the persuasive nature of a promotional email.

Email is like broadcast for its immediacy of response, yet it's much less expensive. Measuring the online response to email is a matter of course. Measuring the offline response requires an extra step. Measuring the offline financial impact of an email promotion is where the best marketers shine.

THE STORY

ED EXPECTED TO FIND a tough bean counter when he walked over to the CFO's office. Instead, he found an energetic woman with a friendly smile. "So *you're* Ed!" Penny said with her hand out to shake his. "Sorry for putting you off until this afternoon, but I had reports to finish. Leo told me he was impressed."

"He did?"

"Whatever you did, keep doing it. Just soften your delivery a little," she laughed. "I'm about to eat lunch, but tell me, how can I help?"

Ed explained about the service departments, how he wanted to use email to promote the more lucrative services and downplay the money-losers. But he needed a way to track it through the accounting system, not just through the Web site.

Penny looked thoughtful. "You need some background info."

"What do you mean?" asked Ed.

"Last year, we did a profit analysis along the lines you're thinking. We got rid of repairing flat tires. It was a huge amount of our business and we charged $5. But between the labor, the inventory, and the overhead, it was costing us $6 each time. So we stopped."

"Sounds prudent."

"Prudent. I like that. Good word. The problem was that people stopped coming in altogether. We turned them away when they wanted a flat fixed, and they wouldn't come back when they needed other work done. So, we started the flat repair service again, and raised the price to $8. The attrition stopped, but things haven't improved enough. That's why we're thinking about shutting down the service centers completely. How can email help us out?"

"Well," said Ed, studying the ceiling, "Right now we don't know the best way to increase service revenue. It could be to make a direct pitch for it—say, to upsell customers from a basic job to a more expensive one. Or, it could be to drive traffic to the stores for another reason, and then get service work indirectly—a cross-sell.

"We could run email tests in a few cities, across several service departments. The tests would evaluate the appeal of different special offers, to see which offer brings the most people to the service counter and produces the most sales. Then we'll know which one to roll out nationwide."

"And how do you track all this?" Penny asked.

"I can track part of it with our email marketing system, but I'll need your help at a certain point. On my end, we'll monitor of how many people we sent a particular message, how many were successfully delivered, and then how many opened. Trends in click-throughs and other web page visits might also be important—but we don't want to get too hung up on the details."

"Whoa!" Penny interjected. "I'm a detail-oriented person. If email's so great for tracking results—and you've got to know that some folks are skeptical of the results you're promising—why wouldn't you care about the details?"

Ed explained. "Well, for a whole slew of reasons. The technology behind email isn't a perfect science—if you were to monitor the results of the same campaign with two different analytics programs, you'd probably come up with two somewhat different sets of numbers. So many things can skew the resulting metrics: mail servers don't always communicate correctly, people change addresses, some mail gets blocked as junk, and so on. And it gets even more complicated when you try to track where people go on your Web site.

"So, when faced with an imperfect metric such as 'delivered' or 'opened' messages, the best approach is to remember that the final numbers aren't critical. All that matters is the difference between the current results and the previous results."

Penny's face lit up. "Are there any big changes one way or another that are noteworthy? Are the decisions you're making helping or hindering the response rate?"

"Bingo!" Ed was delighted. "So, the first part's easy. Do they open and read the email? Do they click through to the Web site? Do they check out the store locator and do they make an appointment? When they show up, do they mention the email promotion or do they bring a printed coupon from the site? Or, do we simply see an increase in service jobs that's beyond the normal weekly fluctuation? But the trickiest part is next, and I'll need your help. How soon can you turn the profit numbers, so we'll know whether the email has had an impact on service department profitability?"

"On the fifteenth of the month we have the numbers for everything up to the end of the previous month," Penny explained.

"So if we send out the emails by the fifteenth of this month, we'll be able to see two weeks worth of impact in your next set of reports. That'll give us a clue."

Penny looked doubtful. "Derek has always told me that direct mail offers take months to play out. People get our flyers and leave them on the garage workbench for weeks on end before bringing them into the store."

"One of the differences between postal mail and email is that the people who are going to respond tend to do it right away. We can also get Derek to kick it up a notch in the copywriting and expiration-date department."

Penny gave Ed a full-on smile. "You do your magic and let me do mine. I'll start by getting a few months worth of historical data together so we have a benchmark." Ed knew he'd found a key ally at Acme Bikes.

Fundamental Email Marketing Metrics

Total Sends

The number of email addresses to which you attempted to send your message.

Successful Sends

The number or percentage of messages successfully delivered.

Hard Bounces

Messages that are undeliverable due to permanent problems with the addresses, such as they do not or no longer exist.

Soft Bounces

Messages that are temporarily undeliverable due to transient problems, such as full mailboxes or troubled mail servers.

"Missing-in-Action" Messages

A number you may never pin down, but exists nonetheless. Some anti-spam software will accept mail, filter it, and then quarantine messages that appear to be spam. Neither the sender nor the recipient may be advised that the mail was effectively deleted.

Tracked Opens

Messages opened using an email client that can read HTML. "Unique" opens will eliminate duplicate measurements if the same recipient opens your email twice.

Estimated Opens

The approximate total number of opens, based on the measured number of tracked opens (from HTML-enabled clients). Some email marketing software will estimate the number of opens you received from recipients with text-enabled clients.

Tracked Clickthroughs

For messages that include trackable URLs, the number or percentage of clicks on those URL. "Unique" clickthroughs will not include multiple clicks on the same URL by the same recipient.

Forwards and Referrals

Forwards are messages passed on by list members to non-members. Referrals are trackable invitations sent by list members to non-members, facilitating new subscriptions. Monitoring these metrics allows you to gauge the viral effectiveness of your email publication.

"YOU CAN'T DO THAT." Derek insisted.

Ed didn't like being cut off in the middle of a sentence, but Derek hadn't said more than two words to him and those had been limited to "Good morning" and "Good night." Derek had been such a recluse, Ed hoped this was the chance to draw him out.

"Which part needs help?" he asked.

"You cannot deliver an offer like this on Friday that is only valid until Tuesday afternoon," Derek said. "They won't respond. They can't. There isn't sufficient time."

"Yeah," Mark chimed in half-heartedly. "We ran into that about a year ago when we were trying to time a mailing for the Fourth of July. It just didn't work."

"Email's different from direct mail," Ed assured them. "People act fast. And, if they want to take advantage of our special offer, they *have* to act fast. If nothing else, it gets our name out in front of them for next to nothing from a cost perspective."

"Quite right from a branding and awareness perspective—however, you *will* run into trouble doing this for a promotion." Derek held Ed's eyes steadily.

Mark spread his hands. Ed felt his blood pressure rise, but then realized he was trampling all over the direct mail maven's territory. "Derek, it's pretty clear that I'm going to need your help. Can you spare me about a half an hour tomorrow morning so I can tell you what I'm trying to accomplish and get your input?"

Mark nodded at Derek. Derek allowed as how he might be able to make the time.

"HERE'S THE THING about email," Ed explained the next day. "It's fast." He laid out a recent mailing report. *(Figure 4.1, p.34)*

"See, here are stats for the number of people who opened, clicked, and looked at more than three pages from our last mailing. Within three days, it's over."

"You are showing me a report about the receiving and reading of email, are you not?" asked Derek.

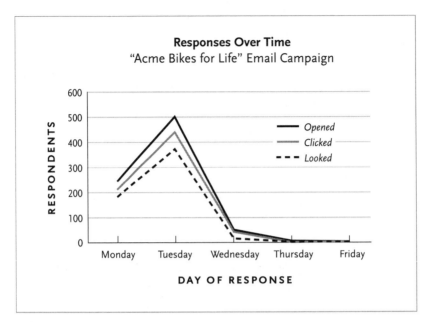

FIGURE 4.1

"Yes..."

"People read your email the day you send it?" Derek asked.

"That's what this report shows. It's not like direct mail where they have something sitting on their kitchen table; they can simply click. They can respond immediately. And if they don't, there's a good chance that they'll delete the message, or file and forget it."

"So you see my point."

"Uhm..." murmured Ed, "I'm afraid I don't."

"Nothing to fear," said Derek. "The typical email call to action is a clickthrough. In this case, the action is a visit to the service department. How do you picture the recipient responding to your email?"

"Well, the message includes directions for clicking through to the landing page so they can find their nearest service department, and print out the coupon."

"Precisely. This brings us to my point."

Ed realized he'd have to start listening to Derek a little more closely. "The coupon," he acknowledged.

"Precisely. An electronic coupon, once printed, will faithfully duplicate a direct mail promotion. It will sit, inert, on the kitchen table, waiting to be snatched up and whisked off to the bike shop, which may or may not happen before end of day Tuesday."

"Ahhh," said Ed.

Derek continued. "Additionally, the message asks them to find their nearest service department. You, however, are segmenting these messages by ZIP code and therefore already know the three nearest service departments. You need not make them search."

"Well," said Ed. "Looks like I was absolutely right."

"Hmm?"

"I *am* going to need your help."

SUMMARY

- The results of an email marketing campaign are not informative until you compare them to those of a previous campaign. Do your best to ensure multiple campaigns are close enough in kind, style, and desired outcome to be comparable.

- Tracking both online and offline results from email-driven marketing campaigns may require collaboration with several different stakeholders; make sure your initiatives have the operational support you'll need from IT, Customer Service, Sales, Finance, and any other marketing groups that may be involved in the process.

- Email may be nearly instantly gratifying, but offline events still require time to unfold. Allow your campaign recipients sufficient time to respond.

WORKSHEET

- What offline actions or events do you wish to encourage? What email-driven incentives can you offer to motivate your audience to take those actions?

- How will you measure the outcome of your online campaign and the resulting offline actions? Beyond technology, what other tools or resources will you need in order to record the results?

CHAPTER 5

Email: Crystal Ball for Sales

KEY CONCEPTS

Forecasting is critical. Most sales organizations live and die by their forecasts. Individual salespeople forecast their monthly and quarterly sales. Managers roll those numbers up into regional sales figures, and upper management tells Wall Street or other investors what to expect.

Some organizations can only forecast retail sales based on history. If sales of Widget X were up five percent for three periods in a row, then it might be reasonable to estimate that they'll go up another five percent in the next period. Production, marketing, staffing, compensation, and other possible expenditures all depend on these fuzzy numbers.

The alternative is to interview a statistically significant sample of prospective customers and correlate their buying propensity to actual sales. Over time, you can get pretty good at it. But unless you're selling billions of dollars worth of household consumables, the cost of face-to-face interviewing is overwhelming.

Email can be an effective forecasting tool. Direct mail has been another useful indicator of audience response, but email has come to the top of the heap from a price-performance perspective. An in-house mailing list is inexpensive to use, the responses to sales offers or questionnaires generate results in mere days, and the ability to run inexpensive tests is a life-saver. As a consequence, email represents one of the best ways to learn from your customers and form opinions about your prospects.

THE STORY

"PENNY, WHEN I TOOK THIS JOB, I was told that this company sells bicycles direct to consumers online." Ed looked decidedly disgruntled.

"We do. You can go look at the shopping pages yourself. I'll bet you even have some ideas that would make them better."

"But how many do we sell?"

"We've only started online sales a few months ago. People aren't used to the idea of buying a bike from us. Besides, they want to ride it for themselves before they buy it."

"But how many do we sell?"

Penny rolled her eyes and turned to her keyboard. "Seven."

"Today?"

"Nooo..."

"Since...?"

"We started about three months ago."

"And how come we've only sold seven?"

"People aren't used to the idea of buying a bike directly from us."

"And we're not used to selling directly to them."

"Right."

"So why did we create an online shopping basket and all the trimmings? Why not just have the dealer locator and leave it at that? Why bother creating something that nobody wants to put any effort into?"

"Because Tony said he wouldn't work here if we didn't."

"Who's Tony?"

"The CEO's son. He's in the process of wrapping up his MBA and slated to take over for Victoria if she takes early retirement. Leo thinks the sun rises and sets on Tony. If you make Tony look good, Tony gets the credit. If he screws up, you get what rolls downhill. Tony pressed for direct, online sales, so..."

Ed finished her sentence. "So we have a shopping cart and order processing system, and nobody wants to work like crazy to make Tony look good."

"Exactly!" Penny responded.

"But Tony's right, and everyone's annual bonus depends on it. Besides, it's great that we've only sold seven bikes so far."

"Why is that great?" asked Penny.

"We need to boost low-end sales, right? And here we have this great channel that's in place but untapped!" Ed said.

"And you're going to tap the wellspring of sales and cause the money river to flow through our Web site?"

"You bet—and I can prove it."

IT TURNED OUT THAT meetings with Leo were not all that common during the intervening months. It was now two weeks before the end of the quarter, and Leo had called the entire marketing team together for a two hour session. The others were nervous about Leo having that much time to paw around their programs. It did not bode well.

Ed arrived right on time. Leo took one look at the stack of binders Ed had prepared for the meeting and started in on him. "You know son, I'm a bit wary of a boy who hides behind reports."

"I've never been to one of these meetings before and I just wanted to be prepared."

"A prepared man's got everything he needs in his head."

Victoria and Derek stepped in, followed soon after by Ava and Mark.

People settled into their seats as Leo started dishing out the bad news. "Sales are *not* where they need to be. The Gold Standard's numbers ain't what they was cracked up to be, the service departments ain't gonna last out the quarter, and the prospect of y'all gettin' bonuses is shrinking along with the sales of our Silver Dollar. So I've carved out a couple of hours this morning to figure out what the heck you're doin' and why it ain't workin', and what the heck you're gonna do about it." There was a pause.

"Well?" Leo taunted.

All eyes turned to see whom Leo had targeted and then swiveled back down to Ed.

"I think things are going quite well," Ed said lightly.

Leo didn't take it that way. "Son, by now the Gold Standard number should 'a topped a quarter of a million, and it ain't cracked two hundred thou'. Service departments are history by this time next month, and low-end Silver Dollar sales are flat, flat, flat. If you got good news—and I mean *any* good news—now would be the time to share it. And don't show me stacks of reports."

"OK." Ed rose to the challenge. "In a nutshell, then. Due to the advertising Ava's been doing, interest in the Gold Standard has increased 15% per week over the past six weeks. Service department visits are up 20% since Derek started his new direct mail campaign, and the Silver Dollar will double in sales in the next two months if current trends continue."

"I don't care if people are interested, I only care if they buy."

"The type of interest they're exhibiting on our Web site points to higher sales."

"I s'pose you can tell what people are thinkin' by watching 'em click?"

"It's the best way we have to forecast sales." Leo frowned. Ed continued, "Extrapolation of previous sales trends is good, but it only predicts the future by looking at the past. Watching how people respond to promotions and where they go on the Web site shows us what's different between this week and last week, and what those people are likely to do in the future." Ed paused.

Leo stared Ed down and shifted gears. "I told you it'd take four percent more net profits by the end of the quarter to keep the service departments alive."

"Penny!" Leo bellowed and the room came to a standstill for a minute while they waited.

Penny came to the door, cocked her head at Leo, and raised her eyebrows. "What's the net increase in service department profits for the quarter?"

"Three and a third percent," she said.

"See?" Leo said to Ed, "The prepared man has everything he needs in his head. That's two weeks, son, and I don't see a thing tells me enough people are gonna be spendin' enough more profitable dollars in service departments in the next two weeks to hit four percent. D'you?"

"Nope."

"But if I'm not hard of hearing, you just said everything was *Jim Dandy*!"

"Given our current growth path," said Ed, "we'll not only hit that four percent in four weeks from today, we'll hit five percent in three months and six percent in six. That should take care of the extra two weeks we were below the four percent you were after this month."

Leo's expression was flat.

"Or you can cut the program now and lose out on those future profits." Ed suggested.

Leo looked at Penny. "Is he right?"

"He's right."

Ed smiled at Penny, and then turned his smile on Leo.

"If you ain't, I'm takin' that missed profit outta your salary." Ed stopped smiling. Penny went back down the hall. "And I s'pose you've got the same thing to say about the low-end line?"

"Yes, I do. There's detailed results in these reports that'll show how..."

"I said I don't want to see no detailed reports, son, and I mean it. You can't..."

"But I do," came a deep voice from the spot where Penny had been standing.

Suddenly Leo was all smiles, a new man. "How the heck are ya? When did you get in? You gonna join your mother and me for dinner? You got time for a chat right now?"

"Great," Tony said with a smile as he acknowledged the others around the table, "I got in just now, yes on dinner, and yes on the chat. Then, I really do want to see those reports."

SUMMARY

- Identify behavior that signifies a prospective buyer by reviewing the online actions your customers took. Then you'll be able to recognize that behavior in your prospects.

- If you haven't used email to promote all aspects of your business, consider using it to stimulate areas that are underperforming—you may be pleasantly surprised.

- Know your numbers, cold—especially if email marketing isn't well understood in your organization.

- Make sure that your Sales, Fullfillment, and Service departments are advised appropriately of your email campaigns, so that they're prepared for any resulting changes in demand.

WORKSHEET

- When you conduct an email campaign that includes links to your Web site, what kind of feedback can you get about the resulting Web traffic?

- Which visited pages—or combinations of pages—are indicative of a Web visitor making a purchase?

- If your business sells its products or services offline, are you able to correlate online behavior with subsequent offline purchases?

- What actions do your Sales or Customer Service departments take when a Web site visitor exhibits behavior predictive of a purchase?

CHAPTER 6

Linking Online Promotions to Repeat Sales

KEY CONCEPTS

Email impacts short-term customer value. The role of email in the sales process can be as simple as inviting people to click through to your Web site and make a purchase. Or your email message could include a purchase form and "submit" button itself, thus streamlining the process further. But things are rarely that simple for most of us, which is why it gets very interesting to track the value of an email promotion as it goes beyond a single sale.

Email also impacts *lifetime* customer value. If you're not thinking about your customers' actions after that first sale, you're probably leaving money on the table. Email raises awareness, prompts actions, and initiates a sequence of events that are difficult to relate back to the original message—but with proper data capture and analysis, you *can* follow an individual customer from that first message to the first sale, and then to the next and the next. When you design your email campaigns with lifetime value in mind, and then manage your tracking accordingly, you'll be making a stronger impact on your business' bottom line.

THE STORY

ED'S PHONE RANG and it was Penny on the other end. "Interesting times," she said.

"Chinese curse."

"And you know the one about chaos?"

"Trouble and opportunity?" Ed replied.

"Very good. The chaos is that Tony and Leo had a few harsh words—indistinguishable, but loud nonetheless, and then things settled down. Tony went directly to Victoria's office, and when he left she was whistling."

"Whistling?"

"She never does that. Right now, I can hear Tony and Mark laughing."

"Laughing? OK Penny, I give up. Spell it out for me."

"This afternoon there's going to be a marketing department meeting with Tony at the head of the table. He's going to want to see your reports. Be ready." She hung up.

MARK, AVA, DEREK, and Ed were gathered an hour later. Mark looked more cheerful than he had in months. Derek looked wary. Ava looked at her PDA.

Tony surveyed the group. "So, I'm just going to lay it out for you. Dad feels like he's losing touch. He doesn't understand what's going on in marketing anymore. He almost gets the Web," Tony turned to Ed, "but he doesn't get the cockiness. He doesn't like the fact that you've shown so little respect, and he doesn't understand what he did to earn your contempt."

Ed drew a breath but Tony held up his hands, cutting him off. "I have now officially delivered the message from the mount. There's one more thing. He's agreed to stop calling you 'son'."

"What? I..." Ed was at a loss for a moment. "I never realized how much that bothered me until just now. Seems like a pretty small thing to lose one's job over."

Tony smiled. "I told him off about that word when I hit 18 and I *am* his son, so you're in good company. And your job is not in danger. Nobody's job at this table is in danger." Eyes darted toward Mark.

"You seem to be pretty sure about your numbers, Ed. Explain them to me so I can assure Dad that all's well in marketing and we can get him back into manufacturing and distribution which is what he knows and loves.

He continued. "Mark already spelled out how you hit the ground running on the messaging and I'm delighted. I mean, I personally really like 'Acme Bikes for Life.' It's very good and it'll work as long as we like. It's timeless. And I'm delighted to see that your research bears it out. So it's a done deal."

Ed nodded, thinking there might be something to the CEO's son after all.

"Next up is the service departments. Dad thinks you're being soft. He wanted to pull the plug months ago, and you want to give it a few more weeks. He's serious about cutting our losses, so tell me, no, *show* me how you reached your conclusions. Where's that stack of reports my father didn't care about?"

Ed woke up his laptop to outline their test and measurement approach.

"There are four things that count when creating a promotion: the medium, the list, the offer, and the creative. The medium is the delivery method. How do you deliver your message? Radio? Television? Direct mail? In our case, we didn't have much time, so the medium of choice was email.

"The most powerful, responsive list of email addresses you can ever mail to is the one you create and maintain yourself. When mailing to our in-house lists of consumers, retailers, and journalists, we can take advantage of all the information we've collected about them. For example, on the consumer and dealer side, ZIP codes can be a good indication of economic status, and past purchase history can be a reliable indicator of future purchase intent."

Ed stopped and asked Tony directly, "Is this the right level of detail? I mean, you must know this stuff, right? MBA and all?"

Tony laughed, "Yes it's familiar, but it's very refreshing hearing it in terms of this company. More importantly, I need to know how much *you* know about all this. Keep going."

"OK, then. Next up are the offer and the creative, and for them I deferred to Derek."

Derek took his cue. "It turns out to be much easier to test offers online than off. If you want to find the pricing 'sweet spot'—say, what works best: $189 or $199—email is the perfect medium. In fact, here's a chart of what we can measure." *(Figure 6.1, p.46)*

"To get particularly subtle, email is a great way to find the difference between 'Buy One Get One Free' and 'Two for the Price of One.' In my research, I read about one retailer whose customers bought more when the online store switched from free delivery to fixed-price delivery. Customers concluded they had already paid for shipping, and that every additional item they purchased represented a discount. But free delivery by itself was simply free, and there was no incentive to drop more items in the shopping cart. The offer that works best is not always the obvious one."

Derek continued. "But even though email makes testing easier, it can get overwhelming. Testing multiple offers against multiple segments, and the inherent complexity of tracking the results, promptly becomes daunting—especially with the introduction of various creative choices. Due to our time constraints, we used our marketing software's segmentation and conditional content tools to test three different offers to 10,000 consumers who live in three specific metropolitan areas."

"What are conditional content tools?" asked Tony.

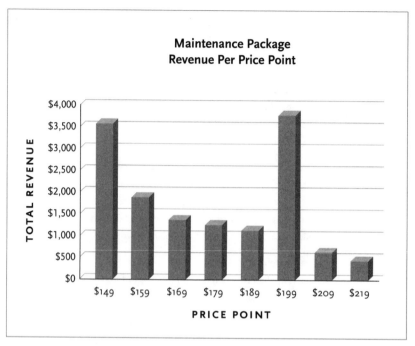

FIGURE 6.1

"They let us program the email system to send paragraph 'A' to some people and paragraph 'B' to others, based on certain conditions they meet. They're very robust and will be pivotal to our email marketing in the future."

"And the results?" Tony was ready to get to the punch line.

Ed responded, "OK. The goal here was to increase the profitability of our service departments. As Derek mentioned, we sent out three different messages, to samples of 3,333 people each." *(Figure 6.2)*

FIGURE 6.2

"Our first message—'Come in to Win!'—promoted a contest to win a new Gold Standard bike. This response report shows that it was a flop." *(Figure 6.3, p.47)*

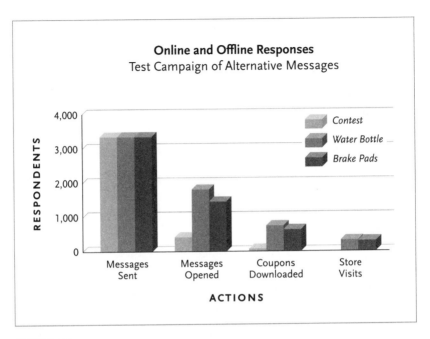

FIGURE 6.3

"I believe that spam filters killed it, and I should have stopped the offer from going out with the word 'win' in the subject line. In fact, our marketing software can test messages for just that sort of red flag, but I overlooked it.

"Of the other two, the 'Drinks Are on Us!' free water bottle offer got the best response—both in terms of message opens, coupon downloads, and store visits. Since we had a couple of extra cases of bottles in the warehouse, this turned out to be a win-win for us, the customers, *and* the bike stores. But it didn't help us in service sales at all.

"Now, the third message was where Derek's work really shined. Derek, explain what you did and I'll show the numbers."

Derek showed Tony and the others the offer for free brake pads that went out with the subject line "Stop on a Dime—on our Nickel!"

"Did you mean free brake pads?" asked Tony. "Why not just say 'Free Brake Pads' and be done with it?"

"Spam filters."

"Right. Sorry."

Derek explained that the pads were free, but the shops would charge for installing them. "Instead of $30 for the whole brake job, consumers only paid $20 and got front and rear pads for free."

"And you're saying we made money on this deal?" Tony was skeptical.

"Short term no, long term yes," replied Derek. "Everyone who visited a store for the brake pad service received a coupon for a discounted annual maintenance package. We tried to make the discount attractive, while still maintaining a decent margin."

Ed picked up the thread. "Derek and Penny tracked those coupons through our service system, and found that about half were redeemed." *(Figure 6.4)*

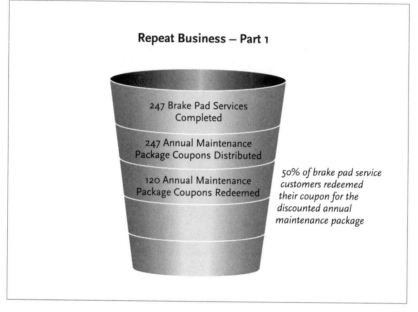

FIGURE 6.4

Tony stopped them. "So now you've run your promotion, but even with those sales, the departments aren't enough in the black to keep them open. Where did you get the feeling that things are going to improve further in a couple of months?"

Derek nodded. "The repeat business goes even further. Fifteen percent of the people who redeemed their coupon for the discounted annual maintenance package came *back* within three weeks with *another* bike needing service." *(Figure 6.5, p.49)*

"*Fifteen* percent? That seems like a lot. Are you sure?"

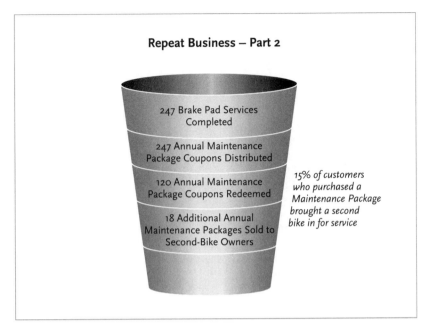

Repeat Business – Part 2

247 Brake Pad Services Completed

247 Annual Maintenance Package Coupons Distributed

120 Annual Maintenance Package Coupons Redeemed

18 Additional Annual Maintenance Packages Sold to Second-Bike Owners

15% of customers who purchased a Maintenance Package brought a second bike in for service

FIGURE 6.5

"Not at first," Mark chimed in. "We doubted it as well, but we verified those numbers across *nine* service departments in the three metropolitan areas. And here's the real kicker, Tony, these increases are based on a set of test mailings done to only 10% of our 100,000-member consumer list. Derek and Ed have yet to roll this email out to the other 90%." Tony was nodding.

"In addition," said Derek, "the original mailing offering the brake pad special only went to one third of that first sample, or about 3,000 people. Every one of the remaining 90,000 in our consumer database will receive that highest-scoring offer."

"And that," said Ed, going to the next chart, "should lead to more than enough business to keep the service departments open. Here's our forecast." *(Figure 6.6, p.50)*

Ed continued. "An added benefit from this campaign is that we collect even more demographic information about the people in our database – how many bikes they own, what kind, and so on. In the future, we'll be able to do even more targeted campaigns."

"You guys definitely have a handle on it," Tony said. "Let me take what I've learned and explain it to my father, then we'll get back together tomorrow to go over the Gold Standard launch." He turned to Mark. "Can we get the whole team together? I'd like PR and Sales here as well."

"I'll make sure that Pearl and Sally will be here."

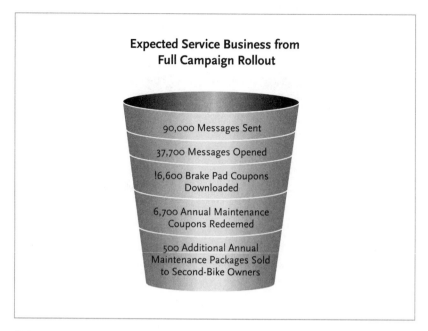

**Expected Service Business from
Full Campaign Rollout**

90,000 Messages Sent

37,700 Messages Opened

16,600 Brake Pad Coupons
Downloaded

6,700 Annual Maintenance
Coupons Redeemed

500 Additional Annual
Maintenance Packages Sold
to Second-Bike Owners

FIGURE 6.6

LATER THAT DAY, Ed was heading home and he stopped by Mark's office. "Got a second?"

"Sure. Are you ready for tomorrow?"

"Yeah, just a couple of questions."

"Shoot."

Ed sat down across from Mark. "What happened to Victoria?"

"Oh, that!" Mark gave a startled smile. "Leo and Tony made her an offer she couldn't refuse, and she is now cleaning out her desk."

Ed's eyes went wide. "Does that mean Tony's coming in?"

"Yep." Mark replied.

"And you're staying?"

"Yep."

"And you understand why I'm confused?" Ed asked.

"Yep."

"And you're going to clear this up for me?"

"Nope."

"Nope?"

"Not until the end of the week. Hang in there and be ready for tomorrow."

SUMMARY

- There are four things that count when creating a promotion: the medium, the list, the offer, and the creative.

- Because email is such a fast medium, it's tempting to make quick assessments of its results. A better approach is to consider lifetime value before calculating the ROI of an email campaign; while a promotion may not be more than break-even in the short term, you could be changing behavior for increased profits in the long run.

- Keep in mind that all customer communications have lasting effects. Make sure your database retains which customers received which offers, and how they reacted to them. You can then create future campaigns based on customer segments with attractive attributes—for example, past purchase history.

WORKSHEET

- How do you monitor and record repeat purchases or other desirable customer actions? What portion of your customer base has made second (or more) purchases?

- What follow-on goods or services can you offer your customers? Complete the table below with several alternatives.

Product/Service Purchased	Repeat Business Offer	Repeat Business Medium	Results Monitoring
Brake pad service	Discount Annual Maintenance Package	In-store coupons	Service-tracking system

- How do you measure the lifetime value of your customers, including the profitability of their purchases? How do your customer service policies—for example, rules for product return or exchange—reflect the fact that customers may make numerous purchases over time?

CHAPTER 7

Capturing Interest and Measuring Perceived Value

KEY CONCEPTS

Know your audience's interests, and deliver them value. Email is a powerful tool for ongoing communications with prospects, customers, the media, investors, and others. But email press releases, newsletters, and announcements can harm your brand just as easily as they can enhance it.

Measuring the public's interest in receiving your announcements and gauging its response to them is one of the simplest email metrics to capture—and among the most important. By monitoring the overall "perceived value" of your messages, you'll gain insights into your brand awareness (is it increasing or decreasing?) and your brand image (how is it changing?).

Testing selected variables leads to powerful results. Along the way, there are more email message variables to work with than are feasible to test. You'll want to limit the number of elements you test so you can be sure which changes you make in your mailings are causing changes to your results. The sooner you can eliminate the variables that have little effect on the outcome, the sooner you can focus on those that make a difference.

THE STORY

AT EIGHT THE NEXT MORNING, Ed was going over some public relations details with Pearl, and keeping an eye out for Sally. He hated to admit that after being with the company for so long, he had yet to meet the Sales Director.

It turned out he wasn't going to meet her until an hour after the meeting started. Since Tony wanted to start with the marketing side of the Gold Standard launch, it was just as well.

"So," Tony started, "have we got a theme for the Gold Standard that's based on the overall message?"

Mark smiled and pointed to a rough illustration showing a cyclist moving very fast down a mountain trail. The headline read, "Live Life to the Fullest—Acme Bikes For Life."

"You tested this the same way you tested the 'For Life' slogan?"

Everybody nodded.

"And you've got a roll-out plan to show me?"

"Well, I guess that would put me and the PR plan first," said Pearl, looking to Mark for confirmation. Mark smiled. Everybody else seemed comfortable with Victoria's absence, but Ed noticed a few eyes checking out Mark for hints and clues explaining his new attitude.

"A couple of years ago, we scrambled to launch the 'Diamond Star' bike, and missed some good opportunities. Ed and I were putting some finishing touches on the contact database just this morning, and the PR rollout is going to be much more effective than before." Pearl nodded to Ed, whose laptop was ready to go, and stood before the projection screen.

"My goal is to maximize the Gold Standard's exposure in all of the relevant press segments. This report shows how we've divided the editorial portion of our email list by area of interest and publication period. The way Ed's set it up, I'm sending out one of nine press release notifications depending on area of interest and publication period. *(Figure 7.1, p.55)*

"Those interested in professional racing who publish once a month," she said, pointing to a column indicating 20 editors, "are going to get the 'Competitive Perspective' announcement 90 days out. The weekly writers will get theirs 30 days out, and the dailies get theirs two weeks in advance.

"There's another announcement for the technical pubs, and another for the sporting goods crowd. I've got draft messages set up to go out automatically when the right dates hit, and we can add new editors at any time. And if an editor changes position or area of interest, or even shifts his publication period, it's a simple update to the database."

Pearl continued. "When any of these folks click on links in the announcement, they go to the Web site's press room. From there, we can keep an eye on what catches their interest.

"If we see a lot of traffic to the testimonials from our sponsored team, we'll get more aggressive about setting up interviews with our celebrity racers. And Ed showed me how I can use our email system's 'triggered mailings' function to automate future mes-

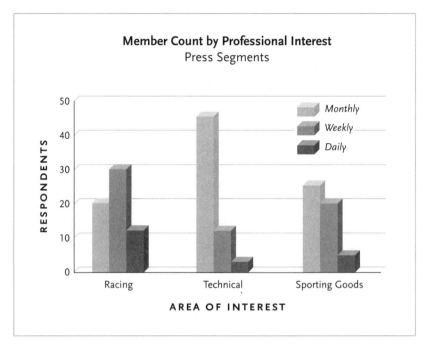

FIGURE 7.1

sages...like when a journalist signs up for our "Extreme Bike-a-Thon" event this fall, her database record will be updated automatically so she receives a follow-up email and press pass one month before it starts."

"And there's even more," Ed chimed in, as Pearl sat down. "We'll monitor all of the publications for press mentions, and then input them into the email system as an association between the specific journalist and the mailing he or she received. That way, we can get an idea of the effective 'ROI' of our press campaigns, and know which press segments are best for Acme Bikes."

"Confidence seems high," Tony said, looking for reassurance from Pearl.

"It's not simplistic, but it is simple. I mean, the steps all make sense; there are just a lot of variables. Get them all lined up and, yes, confidence is high," she answered.

"You've done this sort of thing before, Ed?" Tony asked.

"I've run a few campaigns, and read about many others. It's just a matter of putting the pieces in place, and we have."

"Have you done any testing?"

"A ton," Ed replied. "We've all been recipients of the draft mailings, and so far everything's going according to plan. Our testing has included the HTML formatting, the header fields, the clickthrough links, and all of the tracking variables that are part of the back-end."

"Glad to hear it. And what's happening on the direct side of things?" Tony replied.

Derek began to explain. "We're going to launch a postal mailing to targeted members of our in-house consumer database, and to bike enthusiasts on several rented lists as well. Those rented lists probably won't be as effective as our own list, but we have another goal beyond promoting the Gold Standard, which I'll get to in a minute.

"The direct mail campaign will consist of postcards announcing a contest to win several different prizes—a free Gold Standard, for one. To enter the contest, recipients just need to visit our Web site and register; if they're not already a member of our opt-in newsletter list, they'll join it through the contest registration process."

"We're going to track this campaign in three ways," Derek continued, going to the screen. "First, we'll monitor contest registrations, and see how they compare with similar campaigns we've done before. Next, we'll watch our newsletter list's subscription rates, to see if there's a net increase in membership once the campaign is underway. Take a look at this chart." *(Figure 7.2)*

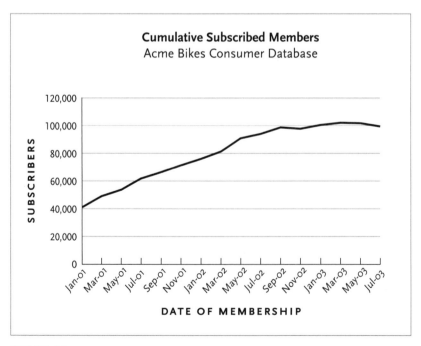

FIGURE 7.2

"You can see that we've hit a plateau this year." Derek drew a bracket around the last five months. "Our list grew quickly a couple of years ago, but at the moment, new subscriptions are barely keeping pace with attrition. Our churn rate nullifies our efforts to grow the list further. We'll be monitoring this trend closely, to see if people join the list and then unsubscribe from it once their contest registration is complete.

"The third metric focuses on the recipients' response to our newsletter. They may..."

"Just a second." Tony interrupted. "Before you go on, walk me through the churn issue so it's crystal clear." Derek turned to Ed.

This was Ed's home turf. "True opt-in means that we make an offer to send email of value in exchange for a subscription. We then measure how many people sign up and stay on the list. We want to know if we can boost subscriptions and lower the number of unsubscribes by describing the newsletter one way or another, or promoting it in different places, or including sales or service incentives of some kind.

"One of the best measures of the value of each newsletter is how many people subscribe or unsubscribe after each mailing. Faithful readers will stick with us through thick and thin, and the best of them will forward our newsletter to their friends—who may themselves sign up. The rest, however, are as fickle as can be and may unsubscribe at the first dip in interest. On the bright side, if we have talented writers and deliver value with each message, we'll see subscriptions going up with every delivery."

Tony looked doubtful. "I get any number of newsletters that I don't necessarily read, but I don't unsubscribe from them either."

"This is one of those fuzzy areas," Ed acknowledged. "There are people who simply can't be bothered to unsubscribe. They might prefer to never hear from us again. It's just that they're busy right now, so they simply delete the message. Maybe they'll have time next week or next month and will unsubscribe then. Maybe. It's just one of the noises in the signal-to-noise ratio that you live with."

"But Ed, that might result in a database filled with non-readers," Derek pointed out. "Is there a data cleansing service similar to those used for postal databases?"

Ed replied, "There are some change-of-address services, to help list owners try to keep their membership current. And I've heard that some companies dump their entire house lists from time to time. They send out several warnings: 'If you do not reply to this email, you will be deleted from our database.' It's a drastic step, but results in a very clean, dedicated membership list. The drawback is that they end up deleting people who read sporadically, but are nonetheless interested. I can't see us going that far at this point."

Tony wanted to be sure he was following the conversation. "So while you're trying to keep a clean list, what are you doing to encourage the majority of readers to stick around? And how do you get more people aside from postcards?"

"We have a whole host of ideas to get current subscribers involved in the brand, rather than simply living on the receiving end of our promotions," Derek revealed.

"Such as? Give me an example or two," asked Tony.

"Surveys, polls, customer stories, repair tips, digital photo of the week, contests, local events—that sort of thing."

Tony nodded as Derek continued. "In essence, we reposition direct mail to funnel people to the email system, using the email system to funnel people back to the Web site...and, ultimately, into the stores." *(Figure 7.3)*

FIGURE 7.3

"That's the third way you're going to measure direct mail?" Tony asked.

"Precisely. We test the market via direct mail with a few ideas to see which resonate. We then track responses to the e-newsletter, and track readers' interests from one page to the next. What we learn from their responses will be fed into the subsequent rounds of advertising. Perhaps Ava can fill you in."

"Yes, I'd like that in just a minute, but first I want to understand what you mean when you say you're going to measure people's reactions. Are they going to fill out a survey every time you send them a newsletter?"

"Nothing so intrusive," Ed assured Tony. "There are a whole bunch of things, recordable things, that people can do, that we can capture, count, and compare from one message to the next."

"OK, so start me off with a single message—no, make that two. You send out two messages and you capture information about people's reactions. What are you measuring and why are you measuring it?"

"Exactly!" Ed grabbed a stack of papers from the table. He'd been waiting for somebody to ask the right question. "But let's look at it the other way around. First, what elements *can* we compare from one message to the next?

"Here's an article I wrote about six months ago that describes the various components you can measure." He passed the article around, and gave them a minute to scan the introduction. (*Figure 7.4*)

Testing, Testing...1, 2, 3

Are you using email for marketing? Good.
Are you testing the success of your emails? Excellent.
But what are you testing?

When using email for moving people into and through your sales pipeline, you have a variety of variables to exploit. There are so many variables, in fact, that their mere contemplation can become overwhelming quickly. But don't panic: managing the process becomes much easier once you review the alternatives and make some thoughtful choices.

1. The Medium
2. The List
3. The Offer
4. The Creative

The Medium...

FIGURE 7.4

"That's a lot of variables to choose from," Tony said, after turning several pages. "Let's take a break, and meet after lunch. In the meantime, I'll read through the entire article. But would I be right to assume that Derek's dexterity in creating offers and writing grabbers is where we're focusing?"

"That's our plan!" said Ed. "As you'll see when you read the rest of the piece, it's important to select a manageable number of variables to test. We're primarily interested in identifying the offers and creative approaches that resonate best. And we need to keep in mind, always, that the specific results from those tests aren't as important as how they compare against the results of other, similar tests. *Relative* performance is paramount."

Testing, Testing... 1, 2, 3

Are you using email for marketing? Good.
Are you testing the success of your emails? Excellent.
But *what* are you testing?

When using email for moving people into and through your sales pipeline, you have a variety of variables to exploit. There are so many variables, in fact, that their mere contemplation can become overwhelming quickly. But don't panic: managing the process becomes much easier once you review the alternatives and make some thoughtful choices.

Direct marketers know that there are four main areas that count when creating a promotion:

1. The Medium
2. The List
3. The Offer
4. The Creative

The Medium

Email is the medium-of-focus here; others include print, telemarketing, radio, television, and outdoor, such as billboards.

The List

Lists can either be built in-house over time, or rented from list brokers when a special need arises. Building your own list with a double opt-in process will typically result in a very solid membership; these people have willingly joined your list, and therefore are more likely to want to hear from you.

Renting email lists is essentially the same as renting postal mailing lists with one major exception. Like direct mail lists, some are more current, some are more targeted. Some produce better results for unknown reasons. Most offer selects based on a variety of factors allowing you to send only to people meeting specific criteria and all allow you to send test messages to subsets in order to test the variety of variables covered here.

The one way in which email lists differ from postal lists is the severe backlash you can expect if you rent the wrong email list and are accused of spamming. Any references made to email list brokers in this article are intended to mean vendors who provide fully vetted, double opt-in lists only.

There are two levels of testing to consider when renting addresses from a list broker. First, you test each list against each other; then, you test other variables within the best-performing list.

For example, find three different lists that look like your target audience and send your message to 1,000 addresses from each of them. Which list gets the best response? Which generates the most subscriptions, registrations, sales, etc.?

Once you've identified the best-performing list, test other variables within it. Some list owners offer selections by category of interest, age, geography, job title, gender—just like the postal list managers. By slicing that best list into three categories, you can test which selection set is the mostly likely to respond to your message. Then you can open your wallet and unleash your message to the bulk of addresses in that list in that selection set.

The Offer

There are thousands of potential offers you can try. Free delivery, first three months free, 30% discount, free trial—you name it. The complexity of testing immediately becomes apparent given the permutations.

What if you only had three offers and you were going to test them against three lists? You suddenly have nine different mailings to track.

	List A	List B	List C
Offer X	1	2	3
Offer Y	4	5	6
Offer Z	7	8	9

Keep the number of offers manageable, because there are quite a few other variables you're going to have to juggle.

The Creative

You're going to use email to send a specific offer to a specific list of recipients. How are you going to describe that offer? What graphics might you use? What verbal imagery might make people click to buy?

Decisions about creative revolve around brand, style, and tone. Your creative options include the color of the background, the size and choice of the font, and even the use of allegory and metaphor.

When he posted to the UK-Netmarketing list (www.chinwag.com/uk-netmarketing) in October 2001, David Cabrera of Aura Corporation (www.auracorp.co.uk) offered the following view of the power of these components:

> Targeting—600% difference between the best and worst lists
> Incentives—400% difference between the best and worst incentives
> Creative—35% difference between the best and worst creative
> Response Device—15% difference between best and worst
> Timing—10% difference between best and worst.

So now we have three lists, three offers, and an infinite number of creative variations. Even if we limit our creative choices to three, we just bumped up the number of testable combinations to 27 or 3 x 3 x 3.

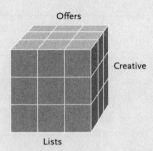

The trick is to balance the need for testing accurately with the desire to change too many things at once. In a scientific laboratory, one learns to test only one variable at a time. In an ideal marketing environment, you'd send out the first piece and measure the results. In the next iteration, you might change the creative—say, a different background color—and measure the results. Following that, you could change the offer and measure *those* results. If you worked this way, several things would happen:

1. You'd learn exactly which changes had exactly what impact on your efforts.
2. You'd run out of email addresses.
3. You'd run out of marketing budget.
4. You'd aggravate your colleagues and boss to no end!

Given that, you need to be selective about your test elements and your test process. There are many creative choices, a sample of which is listed below.

Format/Layout

Email comes in numerous flavors, and we can expect new ones to come along in the future. Within the email medium, you can test ASCII (plain text), HTML (Web page), or rich media (multi-media) to determine which format generates the best results.

Text

Some readers prefer plain text because it's the fastest to download—an important factor for people who travel a lot, for example, who have to access their mail from a relatively slow dial-up connection. Others prefer text because it's so straightforward; the "minimalist" appearance can create a no-nonsense, less (obviously) commercial appearance. Within a text-only message, however, you still face decisions about layout.

Do you send a long newsletter full of complete articles? Do you send a list of articles with links to the Web pages where they can be found? Do you use bullets?

Indent? Provide a table of contents at the top? Each of these choices will depend on the brand impression you're trying to make, followed by the results of the tests you run.

HTML

Most email marketers have found that while only half their subscribers may choose to receive an HTML format when offered a choice, the clickthrough rates of those recipients are much higher. The same question of layout applies, but with a few more choices. Color, graphics, links—all the elements of a Web page come into play and slight changes can make big differences.

Is your message complete or does it include active calls back to the server to download content when the message is opened? Is the response mechanism included or does it require a click to a response page? Does your design use stylized images or photographs? Does the message design have its own, unique style, or does it mirror the design on your site?

Rich Media

If an email message can contain full HTML, then it can contain "rich" or "streaming" media as well. How do your prospects and customers respond to an email message with an embedded, streaming video?

To:

How do you address your message? It sounds like a simple question, but there are several choices that may have an impact on your message delivery.

If you send your message "To:" individual subscribers, you have a choice of including their names in that To: field. You can address your message to *jsmith@company.com,* or to *"John Smith" jsmith@company.com.* The latter may help improve delivery to servers with strict anti-spam filters. You might alternatively choose to heighten *your* brand name by addressing the message to *"Your Company Name* Newsletter Readers." If you're sending out a weekly listing of theater events, you might get a better response by using the To: field to declare "XYZ Readers in Albany, New York."

From:

From whom do you send your message? This is another important question related to branding and response, and another variable for testing. Regardless of what you select, it's important to use both a "name" and an "address" in order to improve delivery to recipients with strong anti-spam protection. Including full addresses is one step to demonstrating that your mail is legitimate.

Individual From: address

Jane Doe <jdoe@company.com> might be appropriate if the author is part of the mailing's appeal. Some newsletters are fun to read because the author has a strong voice. If the message comes across as personal and has personality, you may improve your results.

Organization From: address

The corporate communications department may dictate that your communications come from the corporation and not from a human being. If so, then "XYZ Corporation" may be your only choice for the From: field. Testing will tell you how your customers feel.

List server/hosting provider From: address

Some third-party list management services include their brand name in every message their clients send; if their brand name is well-known and respectable, you might benefit a bit from the "halo effect." Otherwise, it may be worthwhile to step up to a service that allows you to promote your brand exclusively. Also note that some providers of free email services go a step further and toss in advertising from *their* clients. If it's free for you, somebody has to pay the bill.

Is it possible that you'll get a better response from your mailing if your name is not on the label? Anything's possible—that why testing matters.

Subject:

In the direct mail world, you have the entire surface of the envelope to work with. Size, paper stock, texture, color, finish and applied foils and varnishes are at your disposal, not to mention the sheer amount of real estate available for text. Text can change size, shape, color and font, overlap, intertwine, and twist and turn according to the desires of your graphic artists.

The email subject line is significantly different. All creativity is relegated to the words you use, and you have space for only a few. You could use that valuable real estate for a call to action, your company or product brand name, or your newsletter's brand if it's recognizable. What really matters, of course, is which words net the best final results, and you'll only be sure of that by testing.

Date:

The time at which you send your message can impact its success as well.

Time of Day

When do people open their email? First thing in the morning? Just before their first meeting? All day long? Send out a message at 6:00AM Eastern Time and it will be waiting for most U.S. recipients when they turn on their computers for the day. That might be a detriment if your message looks like all the rest; it may simply be deleted in the morning rush to clean up the overnight spam.

Is 10:00AM better? Are you accounting for time zones? Unless you've collected demographic data for your own house list, it's unlikely that you'll know the time zone of all of your recipients. It may seem obvious on paper, but you shouldn't send things out at 4:30PM from California if you want the whole nation to get the message by the end of the day.

Day of Week

Assume Monday's bad. Assume people get more of their mail at work than at home, and that they are inundated with email on Monday morning. Assume that Friday afternoon is bad as well in that people are winding down and likely to leave your message until Monday morning when they are more likely to delete it out of hand.

That said, make assumptions at your own risk. Some messages—or their audiences—are just right for Monday morning. In other scenarios, Friday afternoon might be best for your newsletter to strike a chord with your audience. Try it and see.

Day of Month

Accounting professionals, sales teams, payroll staffers, and a whole host of other email recipients operate under a varying level of tension that typically culminates at the end of the month. They may likely be more willing to read your missive at the beginning of the month when they have more time, or at the end of the month when they have more need.

Other time-related issues

Some periods are best for generating the highest *immediate* response, while others may cause the highest response *over time*. If your message is time-sensitive—for example, last-minute airline tickets—you'll aim for the former. The only way you'll know the "response curve" for a particular mailing time is to test it.

Lastly, there's the matter of handling all of the responses you'll get from your recipients. If you send a message at 6:00AM Eastern Time with the call to action of "Call Now!," will your office be properly staffed to answer the phones? Alternatively, if you offer a limited-time special that expires on a weekend, will purchases on those days be processed appropriately? Make sure that your entire sales or support cycle is prepared to handle the effects of your marketing.

Content

The content of your message also requires you to make many choices, some of which you may only want to make once. Let's start with those variables first, and work through to the ones with which you are more likely to experiment.

Layout

When was the last time you took a critical look at the the design of your HTML or plain text newsletter? Some marketers consider message layout to be a "given" once it's been designed. That stability might be helping you, but you won't know until you test alternative approaches. See if a different font, ASCII border, or style of bulleted contents elicit different responses. That way you'll know if familiarity is working in your favor.

Length

Some news may warrant a short, dedicated message, others may be best communicated as part of a larger piece. To see if length impacts your results, test several versions of the same message. Do clickthrough results improve one way or another?

Tone

What is the character of your communication? Formal, stoic, and professionally dry? Or chatty, fun, and personal? Within the parameters of your brand—image, character, etc.—you can test different tones to see which leads to the best response.

Personalization

Do your readers respond positively to personalized content? For example:

```
Dear Jane:

We hope all is well at your office in Anytown, USA.
In this newsletter, the 37th edition we've sent you,
we're going to cover the following topics:
```

If this style garners more responses than a non-personalized, catch-all salutation, you may want to take advantage of your email marketing software's *mail merge* or *conditional content* tools. If you've collected demographic or psychographic information about your list members, you can send personalized messages to different market segments—for example, women in Georgia who like cats, or men in Oregon who own a dog.

You should, of course, test to see if including additional personalized content—such as references to past purchases, downloaded files, pages visited, etc.—generates higher responses. Be careful not to alienate readers by coming across as *too* all-knowing, as there is likely a limit to what people find acceptable. If highly personalized messages are followed by an unusually high unsubscribe rate, you may have pushed that limit.

Headline and Lead Paragraph

Testing different headlines and leads is important because your audience isn't completely hooked yet; trying alternatives here is also more manageable than testing different versions of your entire newsletter. The headline is the title or the name of your content, and in some cases might be the same as your Subject: line. When creating a newsletter, you might try several titles to see which one motivates readers to continue reading. You'll also want to make sure that your headline segues smoothly into your lead paragraph, so that readers aren't distracted by a possibly confusing digression.

Point of Differentiation

What's special about your offer? What makes it worthy of the recipients' attention? Is it low price, great value, limited time offer, or some other rare and unique element? The message you use to make your offer can not only create varying amounts of email response, it can give you an idea of what the marketplace thinks in general—*if,* of course, your email recipients are representative of that marketplace. If that's the case, you may be able to apply the most resonant email message to other media (radio, television, etc.) as well.

Close/Call to Action

What's your final motivating statement? "Click here to read more" might, in some cases, draw more people back to your site than, "Read more and win a million dollars."

Response Mechanism

Live links are the most common approach and may easily be the best. Giving people the option to reply via email might be more appropriate in certain instances. An entreaty to call today might generate more leads than an embedded submission form.

Reach

How many people are going to see your message? Reach can be expressed as an integer, but it is often discussed in terms of percentages of a given universe. If you sell household packaged goods, such as soap and toothpaste, your universe is just about everybody. If you sell luxury automobiles, your universe is smaller—say, owners of other luxury vehicles, or people with a certain income level.

Frequency

Sending a discount coupon for groceries once a week sounds just about right. A weekly message announcing a new luxury SUV may be overkill. A daily newsletter about the weather is welcome. Alternatively, a yearly newsletter about changes in medical research might be too infrequent for concerned readers.

Landing Page

While the landing page is not technically email, it is a vital part of your efforts. The most common response mechanism is the clickthrough. If your email recipients are clicking through to your home page, you're missing the best chance of measuring your effectiveness as well as your best opportunity to persuade your prospects and bond with your clients.

The same issues you consider when building an outbound HTML document come into play here: layout, color, images, headlines, font style, font size, guarantee, time limit—you name it.

There are page testing systems that can automatically test for the best possible landing page. First, select the variables you want to test—elements such as multiple images, different layouts, alternative headlines, body copy, or the location of all of the above. A page testing system then creates thousands of permutations of the pieces you've chosen by mixing and matching the various components. By serving up different versions of that landing page and measuring the number of people who fill out a form, register for an event, purchase a product, or complete some other action, the system can determine which elements have the biggest impact on the desired behavior and which version of those elements are the best at getting results.

Triggered Mailings

When stored messages are triggered by events, measurement moves beyond a single message and focuses on the aggregate of your communications. This kind of initiative gives you many additional variables to measure, such as the combination, sequence, frequency, and time period of a set of mailings—all of which must be analyzed to identify the ideal series.

Triggers can include downloads of white papers or screen savers, shopping cart activity (e.g., specific items placed in or taken out, cart abandonment, etc.), contacts with customer service, participation in a Web-based poll, and so forth.

What to Test First?

Given all these options, some marketers freeze like a deer caught in headlights and hope that someone else will select the variables to test. But other marketers make decisions like this every day, following one of two general paths.

The first approach is simply based on politics. Who on the team has the most power, or is closest to the final decision maker? That person's preferences—based or not in strategy and reason—may become the game plan through sheer force of personality.

The second approach is to identify your team's strengths. If you have crack designers on board, challenge them to create the most attractive looking message they can; then ask them to do it again and top themselves. Then test the results. On the other hand, you may have somebody who is brilliant at creating offers, or at writing engaging prose. Either way, motivate these people to come up with several, viable alternatives, and then evaluate them with the audience that matters most: your list members.

SUMMARY

- Segmenting your database or mailing list into groups with similar interests or attributes allows you to send more targeted content—which, to a certain extent, should increase the response you get. The degree to which you personalize your messages depends on the relationship you have with your prospects and customers.

- Key elements of membership activity—subscriptions, forwards or referrals, and unsubscribes—are good indicators of the relative health of your list. Any increases in subscriptions due to referrals is a good sign that the perceived value of your newsletter is high.

- Traditional direct mail can do more than stimulate online or offline sales; it can also funnel recipients back into your email marketing system, which can, in turn, direct them back to your site or retail establishments on a regular basis.

- Testing the results of your email campaigns is important for several reasons; among others, you'll be more confident in the results, and you'll be better able to make informed decisions about future campaigns. The number and variety of variables to test, however, is far beyond what most marketers can manage, so you need to be selective. Pick the elements to evaluate based on your resources, skills, and goals.

WORKSHEET

- What metric(s) do you use to evaluate the "perceived value" of your newsletter? What do the results of this measurement indicate about your audience's opinion of your publication?

- How do you/would you personalize your email campaigns? At what point would you limit the personalization and why?

- How do you monitor membership activity? How have your subscribe, referral, and unsubscribe rates developed during the last year? What steps would you take to improve these results?

- What email-related variables would you likely test in a new, upcoming campaign, such as format, subject line, call to action? What others would you evaluate if you had additional resources?

- Complete the matrix below with your proposed lists, offers, and creative components. Mix and match to create the maximum number of combinations that you can practically test and analyze.

List/Segment	Offer	Creative
House list/recent purchasers	*Extended warranty*	*HTML vs. plain text*

8 Driving Interest,
Driving Sales

KEY CONCEPTS

New technology means better integration. As computerized marketing tools become more powerful, it's becoming highly desirable—and feasible—that they talk with one another. As well, new analytics tools are bringing transparency to a discipline that was previously something of a "black box." All of this development and integration creates a more comprehensive view of customers and their activities than we've ever enjoyed before.

Email is one of the foremost media to advance this movement, as it is several things at once: a promotional tool, a retention tool, a survey tool, and a customer service and communication tool. The results of email marketing campaigns can be combined with other marketing metrics to paint a more complete picture of leads, prospects, customers, and the marketplace.

Tracking "interest" means better business intelligence. No longer is it a matter of identifying which promotions raised awareness most, or shifted brand positioning best. We're even beyond connecting promotions to the sales they generated. Now, it's possible to quantify the amount of *interest* a campaign generates in the hearts and minds of your audience, and to measure that interest in terms of moving prospects into and through your sales pipeline.

Once you're monitoring your pipeline, or sales cycle, you'll have a much clearer idea of how email marketing can contribute to your bottom line—all the way from the creation of new leads to the cultivation of loyal, repeat customers.

THE STORY

THE GROUP REASSEMBLED that afternoon, Ed's article on testing thoroughly digested. Tony was ready to bring the conversation back to the task at hand: selling bicycles. "OK, so we can tell how much value we're delivering by whether people unsubscribe, or how many friends they encourage to sign up for our newsletter. Before, you mentioned tracking all the way through to actual sales. Online and offline behavior are all well and good, but I want to see how they relate to people buying bikes."

"The best way to approach email marketing measurement," said Ed as he took a pen from the white board tray, "is by looking at the sales cycle. The sales cycle, the sales funnel, the pipeline—it goes by many names—describes the process of identifying potential customers and turning them into actual customers. I like specific designations for each step in the flow." *(Figure 8.1)*

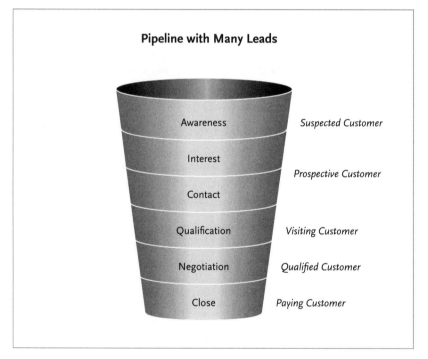

FIGURE 8.1

"People who share attributes with our current customers are the most likely to become new customers, and we call them 'leads' or 'suspects.' In our business, anyone who subscribes to a mountain biking magazine is a lead.

"So we can look at a Web site like 'Extreme Mountain Biking Headquarters Dot Com,' where a million people have signed up to receive commercial email messages about cycling. We can rent membership lists from this site, to use for one-time promotional mailings. Their total universe of leads is 1,000,000. But Acme Bikes can't sell to all of them, because we don't ship overseas, so the relevant universe really only includes 750,000 leads.

"If we were to rent a list and then mail to it, the recipients who respond to Derek's messages by clicking through to the Acme Bikes site would be reclassified from 'leads' to 'prospects.' And at that point, we get into another level of granularity."

Next to his pipeline drawing, Ed wrote the following list as he spoke:

Suspect/Lead
Prospect
—*Visitor*
—*Unique Visitor*
—*Return Visitor*
—*Qualified Visitor*
—*User*
—*Qualified Prospect*
Customer
Advocate
—*Respondent*

"I prefer to define the first level of prospects as 'visitors.' They may only come to our site once, and they may only look at one page, but they've expressed a greater amount of interest than those leads who didn't visit us at all.

"One visitor may come three times over the course of three days, so it's important to distinguish unique visitors—otherwise we'd be triple-counting, and might draw the wrong conclusion about a particular campaign's results. In our case, a thousand people coming to the site once is nowhere near as interesting as a hundred people visiting ten times each. That said, another company might be perfectly content with those single-page visits, if its goal was simply to raise brand awareness."

Ed continued. "The visitor who comes back to our site is infinitely more likely to become a customer than someone who doesn't, so tracking the return visitor is the first step in measuring recency, frequency, and potential monetary value.

"It's all well and good that a unique visitor stopped by 27 times, but if that last visit was four months ago, the likelihood of her becoming a customer gets smaller and smaller with every passing day. Recency matters.

"Bringing lots of visitors to our site through a masterful email marketing campaign may not bring the sort of visitors we want. If Derek offers a gift to everyone who clicks to our site—say, a free $100 gift certificate to an online bookseller—he'll end up with lots of traffic, but only coincidence is going to bring in visitors who care about bicycles.

"Our job is finding those who have a need, who recognize our ability to meet that need, and are financially able to take advantage of what we offer. They are valuable because they are ready, willing, and able to buy. I call these people 'qualifed visitors.'

"The next prospect level is 'users.' People who actively use certain applications on our Web site—for example, a searchable database of cycling events, or a bike configurator—are likely to be more qualified than those who don't. I call attention to these people because they behave differently from those who are simply browsing—they're *actively* involved with us.

"Just beyond them are the 'qualified prospects.' They show all the signs of being ready, willing, and able. They want to buy and we want to sell, so now it's a matter of negoti-ating the contract, closing the deal, or hitting the 'Buy Now' button.

"The first time *that* happens, a customer is born. That person belongs to a unique classification and deserves special care.

"Some customers will make repeat purchases, some even on a regular basis. But even if they don't, they have the potential to become 'advocates' if we treat them right. Advocates will promote our bikes and service—our brand itself—to others. And that's a tremendous asset.

"Beyond the level of advocate is a classification I call 'respondent.' These people may not be the 'best' customers in strictly sales terms, but they offer something else of value: their feedback. Whereas advocates talk about us to others, respondents actively engage *us* directly—about our products, our service, and, again, our brand. They go beyond sub-mitting the Web surveys that we initiate, and write their own, unsolicited testimonials and recommendations. These folks are a rare breed, and give us a direct view of the heart and soul of our customer base."

Ed erased the contours of his pipeline sketch and redrew them with the bulge in the middle instead of at the beginning. "The point of diagramming the sales cycle is to measure how people move through the process from lead to prospect to customer to advocate. If we have a glut of people who are qualified but not buying, we'll know where to focus our attention." *(Figure 8.2, p.75)*

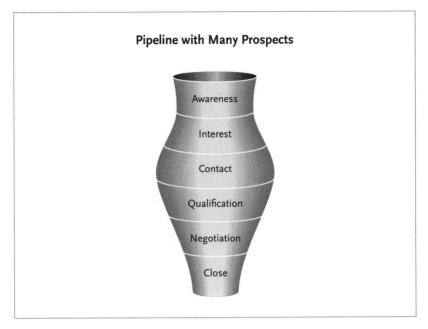

Pipeline with Many Prospects

Awareness

Interest

Contact

Qualification

Negotiation

Close

FIGURE 8.2

"When we solve that problem, we may notice next that there are only a paltry few at the beginning of the cycle. If we don't do something quick to feed more people into the top of our sales funnel, the pipeline will dry up." *(Figure 8.3, p.76)*

"So this gives us a bird's-eye view of the state-of-the-pipeline."

Mark was scratching his head. "I love the visual. It instinctively tells me what's going on—it's a great dashboard. But I'm missing the leap from the information you're capturing to this display. What data triggers the reclassification of a prospect? How do you know somebody is interested?"

"Exactly where I was going," Ed replied. "Given this framework for the big picture, it's time to get down to specifics. Calculating your email marketing success requires two distinct actions: measurement and analysis. Measurement is counting, weighing, and observing. Analysis is the art of comparing those measurements in informative and actionable ways. Your analysis should suggest the subtle changes you can make that can yield large improvements in response and conversion. So, let's talk specifics. Derek, you know this stuff—you take a turn."

Derek took the lead. "When we run a campaign, we know how many messages were sent and how many bounced. We have a feel for how many were opened. If we use tracking graphics—that is, one-by-one pixels—we can tell how many messages have been forwarded."

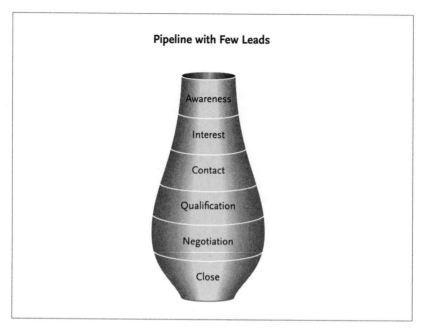

Pipeline with Few Leads

Awareness

Interest

Contact

Qualification

Negotiation

Close

FIGURE 8.3

Tony cocked his head and asked, "Yeah, but if I get a pixel in my email and I forward it, how do you know it wasn't just me, opening the same message several times?"

"By using a non-embedded image that is dynamically, sequentially named inside of each email we send," Derek answered.

Mark wasn't following. "Dynamically? Sequentially?"

Having just learned himself, Derek was able to explain it rather than just name it. "When John Doe opens his HTML email, the message reaches out to the server for an image called '123.gif' and Jane Smith's reaches out for "124.gif" and so forth. If '123.gif' appears in our server log as delivered to ten, twelve or twelve hundred *other* IP addresses, then John is not reading the message again and again. He has sent it on to others who, in turn, have sent it on to others. We have a nice little viral marketing movement on our hands. So it behooves us to keep track of the John Does of the world, and our email software's 'forward tracking' feature lets us do just that. They are the nodes in our marketing communications network. We want to know what makes them tick to keep them exhilarated about spreading our electronic word."

During this exchange, Ed had jumped back up to the white board to make another drawing. *(Figure 8.4, p.77)*

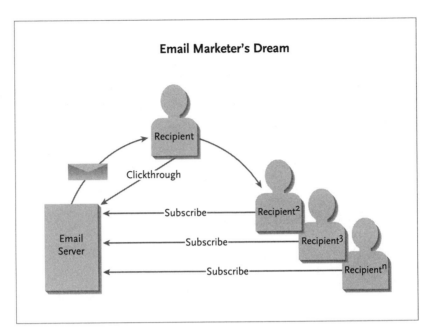

FIGURE 8.4

"Here's a snapshot of what marketers dream about: if our announcements and newsletters are really good, then the people who received them as forwards will subscribe. So we're tracking opens, forwards, and subscriptions so far."

"So far?"

"Yeah. Well, hopefully, we also get the most trustworthy of all metrics: the clickthrough. It's very possible that some people will click on a link in our email by mistake, but we're dealing with large enough numbers that those won't be worth worrying about."

"So," asked Tony. "Do we have some feel for the cost of each click and the value of each click?"

"We can. But it depends on our goals: whether we want people to engage with the brand by coming back to the Web site, downloading a screensaver, configuring a custom bike, or making a purchase. We'll get to that part when we talk about the Silver Dollar low-end bike."

"OK, so they've clicked...what are we tracking next?"

"Visits," said Derek. "Let's consider another company's example. A packaged-goods manufacturer—say, a soft drink maker—wants a nice, long brand engagement. If you go to their site, you'll find online games, contests, greeting cards, and screensavers. When you play their game, send an e-card, or do anything interactive on the site, their marketing managers are thrilled. You might even buy a logoed leather jacket. But you *cannot* buy their soft drinks online. The mere act of visiting is a brand-win.

"Using a combination of email tracking graphics and page tracking technology such as cookies, we can follow the sequence of events from open to click to visit. Consider the following hypothetical example. Messages A, B and C are sent out to a sample of 10,000 addresses from List 1. Let's review the data from message delivery to message opens." (*Table 8.1*)

	Message A	Message B	Message C
Sent to List 1	3,333	3,333	3,333
Bounced	255	156	145
Received	3,078	3,177	3,188
Opened	755	731	802
% Opened	24.5%	23.0%	25.2%

TABLE 8.1

"At this point, we assume Message C is the best candidate for sending out to the rest of List 1, because it was opened the most. But this only shows the very first level of prospect interest. Next, we want to see the numbers for clickthroughs. (*Table 8.2*)

	Message A	Message B	Message C
Received	3,078	3,177	3,188
Opened	755	731	802
% Opened	24.5%	23.0%	25.2%
Clickthroughs	257	245	261
% Clickthroughs	34.0%	33.5%	32.5%

TABLE 8.2

"Message C may have had more opens than the others, but Message A brought in a higher percentage of clickthroughs. It's the one that attracted the most interested people. But just how interested were they?

"One way to frame interest is in terms of visit duration and depth—how long did they stay on our site and how deep did they drill? Assuming longer, more comprehensive visits help us realize our goals, can we alter our offer or our creative to turn an average of three minutes and seven pageviews per visit into an average of ten minutes and 30 pageviews? Alternatively, if we want to make the shopping process more efficient, how can we modify our site navigation to *reduce* the number of clicks or the duration of a visit?

"Only when we combine visit duration with other things—usability studies, brand surveys, and, ultimately, purchases—can we determine whether a longer visit with more clicks helps. More clicks in and of themselves might simply be a symptom of navigational confusion. A visitor looking at 12 pages in one minute might be enthralled, or might be surfing in frustration to find something particular."

Derek went on. "So, we can tell which of our marketing messages is working in terms of generating interest, but how do we tell if they're having an impact on *sales*? How do we tell if we're driving people to the stores—and, at the end of the day, if they're spending *more* money because of their experience with our email-and-web campaign?"

"Sounds like I'm just in time," said Sally, Director of Sales, as she walked into the room and poured herself a cup of coffee. "Where's Victoria?"

"This was an eight o'clock meeting, Sally," Tony admonished, deftly ignoring the second question. "Been closing deals?"

"Been hanging on to retail outlets. Three calls this morning about the Gold Standard launch, and the rumors that we're going to be selling online direct."

"What did you tell them?" asked Pearl, looking worried.

"That we're only going to be selling the low-end Silver Dollar online, because that's what Mark told me, and that we *are* going to use the Internet to sell Gold Standards, but not direct. Each dealer wanted to know how we're gonna use the Internet to send people to *their* stores, and I said I was on my way to a meeting to find out. So here I am. So how's it gonna work? Oh, and you must be Ed. Hi, I'm Sally."

"Good to meet you," Ed smiled, and then looked over to Derek. "All yours."

"I'm comfortable with most of this. Still, I suspect I'll need your assistance before long." Derek turned to Sally. "We were just covering the measurement of our promotional efforts based on email opens, forwards, and clickthroughs."

"My brother runs a Web marketing company. I know all that," Sally asserted. "What I don't know is how you're going to convince Stewart's Cycle Shop to cough up co-op marketing dollars on top of keeping 30 Gold Standards in stock on his nickel."

"You sold him 30?" Tony asked.

"That's what I get paid for," she preened. "So, what do I say to Stewart?"

Derek smiled and warmed to the subject. "You *may* be able to tell him our records indicate he should have 50 Gold Standards on hand to manage the sales he can expect based on the fact that 30% of the Web site visitors in his area have reached an Interest Stage of 60, and that we'll be directing these people to his store from our Web site and email management system."

"That's great," Sally said. "One more time, in English? And what are you grinning about, Ed?"

"Oh, nothing, it's just that this is the good part. You're going to like it." He looked around the table. "You're *all* going to like it." He gestured with an open hand toward Derek.

"If the duration of a visit and the number of pages viewed can mean either a healthy interest or a frustrated visitor, we need a different way to measure interest. We have to identify how specific milestones on our site relate to specific levels of brand involvement.

"The email marketing software we use permits us to monitor the amount of interest our prospects show in our campaigns. The software prompts you to assign numeric values to the levels of interest people show. Let's try a simple example."

Derek started a new list on the white board. "Here are a few actions that our prospects can take to show interest in our business:"

Opt-in	1
Open	2
Clickthrough	5

"When a prospect named Alice clicks through, she immediately accumulates 8 'Interest Points.' She will have opted-in to receive our mail, she will have opened it, and she will have clicked through to a special landing page on our site. Eight points. So far, so good.

"But we cannot award Alice more points merely because she lingered on the site. Perhaps she went to get a cup of coffee, answered the phone, or was interrupted by her assistant. So we assign specific values to specific pages. The highest score might go on the page that says, 'Here are the three retail stores nearest you' or 'Print this coupon and take it to this store.'

"Therefore, Ed and I have created a list of Web pages and their respective Interest Point values. This table helped us to thoroughly document all relevant Web pages in our sales cycle, and made certain that our assigned values were logical.

"Here is the list we developed." Derek passed out a typed sheet of paper (*Table 8.3, p.81*). "If somebody comes to the home page, they have exhibited one point's worth of interest and they are currently at Stage 10 out of 100. Ed, this is your baby—why don't you walk us through it?"

	Page URL	Page Name	Interest Stage	Interest Points
1	www.acmebikecorp.com	Home page	10	1
2	/landing1.html	Landing Page 1	20	2
3	/landing2.html	Landing Page 2	20	2
4	/goldstandard/gallery.html	Photos	30	2
5	/goldstandard/saverthanks.html	Screen Saver	40	3
6	/goldstandard/specs.html	Datasheet	40	3
7	/goldstandard/subscribethanks.html	Newsletter	50	5
8	/dealerlocator.html	Dealer locator	60	10
9	/goldstandard/testrideconfirm.html	Test ride	70	15
10	/goldstandard/reservation.html	Purchase	80	20

TABLE 8.3

"Sure. Derek's already explained Interest Points a bit, but there's another element as well. Interest *Stage* denotes the relative *position* of each web page within our sales cycle. We use a value of ten for those just entering the sales cycle, up to 100 for loyal, repeat customers. Some pages have the same value, because they have similar positions in the sales cycle.

"Consider the sales cycle as a whole and all the Web pages a prospective or returning customer might view in the course of visiting the site. The sales cycle may also include pages that only peripherally support the buying process, like those listing current events, photos, or support policies—anything Alice might look at as she is investigating a Gold Standard.

"As prospects visit different pages, their Interest Stage value will ratchet up to the highest stage value of any page that they have visited. If Alice views a page valued at 50, her stage value will rise to 50 and never fall below that. This lets us gauge the farthest point Alice has reached while viewing the site.

Ed paused to see if everyone was following. "Let's go back to Interest Points. Those values are assigned to particular Web pages to denote the relative *importance* of each page—recall that we gave Alice one point for joining our mailing list, and five points for clicking through to the site from one of our messages. So, overall, we give more points to pages indicating greater interest. In contrast to Interest Stage values, Interest Point values are cumulative. For every page Alice visits, her total Interest Points increase."

Tony interrupted him. "Why are those point values so small? I mean, if Alice went directly to the purchase reservation page, she'd only score 20 points. Isn't she more valuable than somebody who went to the dealer locator twice?"

"Well, in a way, yeah," admitted Ed, "but really large values can drown out the significance of the smaller value pages. We're erring on the side of conservatism. Alone or combined with Interest Stage data, Interest Points tell us which customers are most interested, and allow us to provide them with special offers or treatment or turn them over to the retailer faster. And we can modify the values as we learn more about how interest correlates with sales—for example, if we find a pattern of page views that are typical of a ready-to-buy visitor, we can make sure those pages have stage or point values that stand out."

Ed drew on the white board, and continued to explain. "Here's another scenario that marketers dream about. Many people may open, read, click, and visit. However, the person who comes *back* to our site—either without being prompted, or with a little reminder—is expressing an abiding curiosity in our products." *(Figure 8.5)*

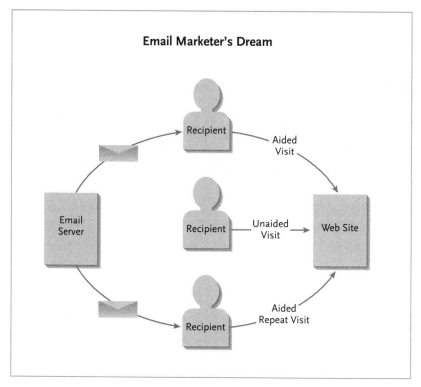

FIGURE 8.5

"Alice may buy a low-priced, impulse item, such as a water bottle or reflector set," Ed went on, "yet must return several times to decide about a fully-loaded Gold Standard. We not only want to track those repeat visits, but also the instances in which Alice comes back on her own 'unaided' volition, without responding to another promotional message."

"So if I'm getting this," said Mark, "Interest Stage ten says Alice has never ventured past the home page—but if she has ten points, she's been there ten times! If we're posting the results of a contest there, she only loves us for the prizes she might win."

"Precisely," said Derek.

Tony's face showed signs of enlightenment. "So, if she's at Interest Stage 70, and has, say, 17 Interest Points, then I'd guess Alice is a woman who knows what she wants. She hit the landing page and went right for the test ride confirmation. No hesitation at all."

"Unless...what if she stops cold on the preceding page and doesn't click the reservation button? She never makes it to the confirmation page," Sally speculated.

Ed responded, "We'll always be watching for moments of abandonment—when people just bail out of the buying process. If Alice has a lot of behavioral company—if the majority of visitors are doing the same—we may be handing out a nasty surprise on that page that puts people off. "

Sally picks up again, "They see that they'll have to drive 100 miles or the page loads too slow or maybe the 'Continue' button is below the scroll line."

"When did you become a Web site designer?" asked Mark.

"When I try buying stuff online and get annoyed every time."

"OK, but what about flipping the points?" Tony wanted to know. What does it mean if Alice is at Stage 40, and has 50 Points?

"Alice doesn't want to buy online, but she's certainly interested. She's scoring way up there in the interest column and is worthy of a phone call or an email."

"We'd have to email or call everybody who comes to our site. We'd need a huge call center," Tony replied.

"We *have* a huge call center," said Sally, finally getting the answer to the question she asked when she came in the room. "It's a distributed call center and it's called retail stores. If hot leads like Alice are automatically sent to dealers for follow-up, we're going to walk all over the competition!" Ed and Mark high-fived, Derek looked smug, and Tony smiled as Sally went on.

"If Alice hits Stage 80 with 32 Points, she's a classic customer. She came, she saw, she purchased. End of story. Nothing insightful, nothing unusual, nothing to get excited about. But if she's at Stage 80, with 65 Points, she's a dream come true. She visits often. She looks at multiple pages. She's *actively* involved in our site."

Ed pulled a report out of his stack and slid it over. *(Figure 8.6)*

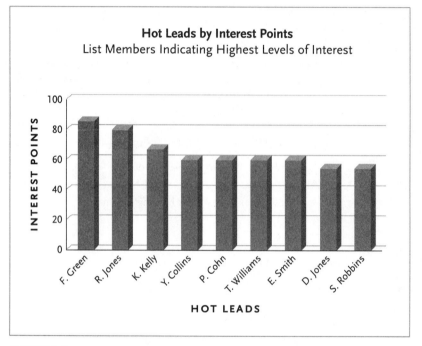

FIGURE 8.6

Sally's eyes went wide as she looked at the report, and then kept talking. "But most important, Alice buys again and again and again. The big deal is that when people like her schedule a test ride or reserve a bike, we'll know which mailings brought in the most people, to the furthest reaches of the sales cycle, at the highest level of interest, in the shortest amount of time. We report that back to the retailers and they'll be lining up trying to do co-op marketing deals. *Nobody* can give them that kind of information about promotions!" She turned to Ava. "And I'll bet you can even tell what's going on with the advertising we're doing!"

"We're working on it."

"Well, why didn't anybody *tell* me this stuff?" Sally demanded. "I've got to make some calls!" And she was out the door.

Mark's eye widened at her enthusiasm and speed. Ed gave Derek a thumbs-up. Tony winked at Mark. Ava smiled into her PDA.

SUMMARY

- Identifying the flow of communication and actions in your business that turns a lead into a prospect into a customer is the first step to defining your sales cycle. Once you've done this, you can start to measure the overall health of your business—that is, the number of people at each stage of your sales cycle.

- Be prepared to generate new leads, make special offers, or take other corrective action when one stage of your sales cycle isn't full enough.

- Measuring the depth or duration of visits to your site is one way to evaluate interest; another approach is to monitor traffic to pages that are critical to your sales cycle, and determine which email campaigns are best at driving visitors to them.

WORKSHEET

- Which pages on your site are typically visited during your customers' shopping process?

- Assign values to the pages you listed above, using the "Interest Stage" and "Interest Points" concepts. Remember: Interest Stage is the relative *position* of a page within your sales cycle, and Interest Points denote the relative *importance* of that page.

	Page URL	Page Name	Interest Stage	Interest Points
1				
2				
3				
4				
5				
6				
7				
8				
9				
10				

- How will you advise your Sales Department of any "hot leads"—that is, mailing recipients who demonstrate a strong interest in purchasing—who come about from a marketing campaign?

CHAPTER 9 Closing the
Feedback Loop

KEY CONCEPTS

The secret to truly successful marketing is *actionable measurement.* Measuring your results alone isn't enough; the key is feeding them back into your sales and marketing processes to make continuous improvements. Many marketing projects fail in this regard.

By the time a marketing campaign has gone from conception to execution, its team's focus is typically on the next project. The best marketers, in contrast, watch their results like hawks—not to pat themselves on the back, but to create benchmarks to beat the next time around. And that's the crux of marketing measurement: you need at least two comparable campaigns to get started.

Your first project serves as a benchmark. Results from your second one will tell you how much better (or worse) you did in comparison. With two projects completed, you're on the road to continuous improvement—remembering, of course, to keep the number of variables under control.

THE STORY

THE ROOM WENT QUIET when Leo walked in and sat down at the head of the table. Six months had passed since Ed had started, six months since the email marketing system had started cranking out some real results.

Leo looked uncomfortable. "I promised Tony I'd keep my nose outta this end of the business for a while, as long as the sales kept coming. I promised Tony we'd make his position here official before too much more time went by. A lot of that depends on what I find out today about how we're goin' about sellin' our Silver Dollar bikes on the Internet.

He continued. "But first, y'all got the memo about the Gold Standard?" Tony and Mark nodded. Ed and Pearl picked up their copies. Sally smiled. Ava looked at her PDA. "Well, I'm real pleased. Sally, you've done yourself proud with those sales figures. I got three calls last week from stores sayin' they'd sold just what you told 'em they would. Good job."

"Leo," Sally interjected, "those stores followed my advice and did well, but my advice came from the awareness groundwork that Pearl did and the promotions that Derek put together. Frankly, the email tracking system kicks out the forecasting all by itself. So I'd say Ed done us proud."

Ed smiled at Sally. Leo squinted at the two of them. "And just when did our Ms. Loner-Closer Saleslady become such a team player?"

"Since I got my last commission check."

"Still paying you too much, am I? Thought so," he said with a wink, but he still wasn't smiling. Something was clearly bothering him.

"You and Penny were right about the service departments, Ed, but you calculated low. I've a mind to open two more before the end of the year, 'cause they seem to be money makers like never before. So good work on that one, so...Ed."

"Thank you...sir."

"But I gotta problem and I need some answers. Tony tells me y'all are makin' this Web stuff work like nobody's business, but I gotta make it *my* business today. I need to know what's happenin' with the Silver Dollar and I need to know every detail. I need to be 100% certain that we're going the right direction sellin' direct.

"I got retailers warnin' me they're gonna walk. I got a warehouse that's gonna be stocked to the rafters. I got orders I gotta place today to hit those numbers in Tony's forecast, and Miss Video Game here wants an ungodly chunk of change for national television ads." Ava put her PDA on the table and looked at Leo with a steady gaze.

"I know Pearl's got the PR roll-out in hand, and I've seen the TV plan. But what I don't see is how we're going to get these bikes off our Web site and out the door. Derek? You and Ed got a good story?"

"Assuredly, sir."

"Let's have it."

Derek walked Leo through the process of tracking direct mail and email promotions from mailing to clicking, and described how Interest Stages and Points were calculated. He was pretty sure that Leo was following him, but he paused just to check.

Leo asked, "What can you tell me about the folks who are interested in the Silver Dollar...say, those got to Interest Stage 50? What do we know about them?"

"We collect standard demographics; ZIP code, age, and gender, as well as some psychographics including the type and frequency of the riding they do. We also record some market analysis elements, like the date of last bicycle acquisition, and the number of riders in the family," Derek answered.

"How'd we get all that?"

"We ask some questions when they register for our newsletter, and others through web surveys."

"They're willing to tell us all that?" Leo was surprised.

Derek looked to Ed, who answered, "They're only willing to tell us a little at a time. This first chart shows that people are willing to answer a few questions, but no more. If it looks like it might take more than a few seconds to answer, they won't." *(Figure 9.1)*

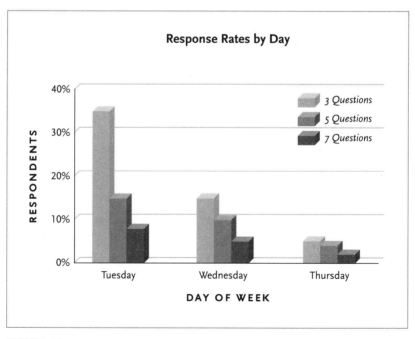

FIGURE 9.1

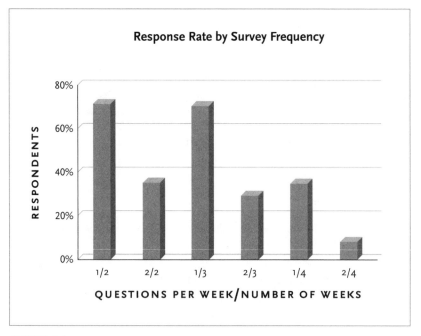

Response Rate by Survey Frequency

FIGURE 9.2

"What's interesting is that people are willing to answer a small number of questions several times." Ed flashed another chart on the screen. *(Figure 9.2)*

"The first column shows that we asked one question a week for two weeks. 70% responded and that's pretty good. But when we asked *two* questions a week, we lost people. What's interesting is that almost the same number of people was willing to answer once a week for three weeks in a row. Two questions per week was a loser all across the board, and people didn't want to sustain the dialogue for a whole month. So, we figure we can ask three questions in a three week period if we deliver value."

"They're willin' to answer questions if you wait a spell, say a couple of months, and then try again?"

"We don't know yet. But we *do* know that we can find out. And to answer your first question, here's what we know about people who've shown interest in the Silver Dollar." *(Figures 9.3 and 9.4, p.91)*

"They have lots of interests, but they're primarily people who like to ride around town, and it's been a couple of years since their last bike purchase. What's reassuring is that these statistics match the market research we did a year ago, when we were planning the product before its launch."

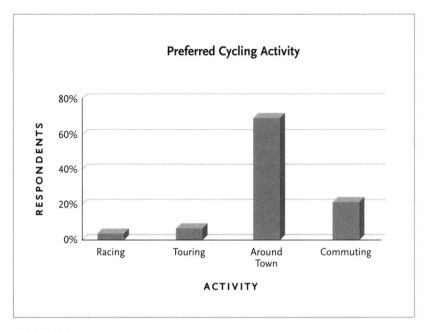

FIGURE 9.3

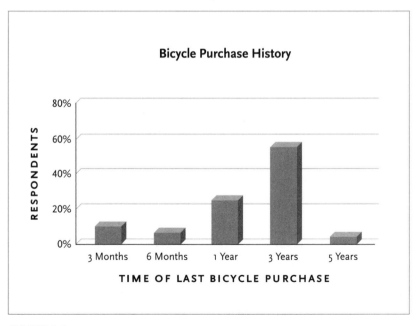

FIGURE 9.4

"Well, I'll be." Leo squinted at Ed and Derek. "So, they're interested. But will they buy?"

"Definitely."

"But how can ya tell, Ed?"

"One of the first things we looked at during our initial test campaign was the people who *didn't* buy; that is, they showed all the characteristics of qualified visitors, but for some reason didn't submit an online order. It may have been because the sales process was too confusing, or because the warranty wasn't enough to convince them to hit the 'Buy Now' button. As we tested multiple email messages, we found that some caused more shopping cart abandonment than others. Here's a good example of one." *(Figure 9.5)*

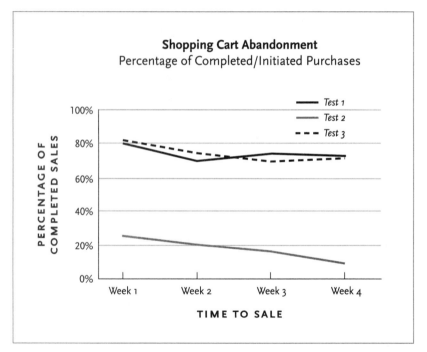

FIGURE 9.5

"The principal difference between these three test messages was in the email copy; the landing pages and shopping cart processes were essentially the same. As you can see, Test Message #2 had a much lower completed sales rate than the others. These results helped us understand that Message #2 didn't manage expectations very well—shoppers were surprised, or confused, by the ordering and pick-up process when they finally reached the online purchase page, so many more of them abandoned their carts.

"From this experience, we learned that honing our messages based on demographics isn't enough—we need to make sure to integrate key elements of those messages through the entire chain of electronic communication," Ed concluded.

Derek explained further. "For example, if a promotional email promises a remarkable price, but the landing page talks about a smooth ride, there's a cognitive disconnect. People tend to abandon when that happens, or at least get very distracted. If the email message proclaims an online discount and the order summary page reflects that offer, more sales will likely be completed. So, over time, we've learned what not to do."

"Right," said Ed. "And we match up the email promise and the landing page pay-off with the demographics and psychographics we collected earlier. The mother of a ten-year-old girl gets a different persuasive approach than a college-aged amateur bike racer. That's called 'conditional content' and we have a surprisingly sophisticated control over what types of people get which types of content in their email."

Then Ed took it to the next level. "See, this is where the investment in the Web site pays off. We're establishing this definitive link between our email marketing efforts, our navigational analysis, and our conversion rates. We're able to connect the cookies and tracking graphics in our email promotions to the cookies and tracking graphics on our Web site to determine which of our email broadcasts has generated the best results. The goal is to measure from the email message to the sale and everything else in between."

Sally couldn't resist, "So we're tracking from point of mail through point of sale."

Tony jumped in, "From clicking to shipping."

"Well, I don't pretend to know a tracking graphic from a two-headed giraffe, but Tony tells me you got a way of watchin' 'em shop that lets you tweak their 'experience' into buying more," interrupted Leo.

"Yes, we do."

"Explain it to me."

"OK!" Ed was no longer hiding his smile at this point. Leo was asking all the right questions, and Ed had some very promising answers.

"All of this applies to every stage of the sales cycle. If Sally were trying to bring new retailers on board, we could apply what I'm about to describe to generating leads for her to close. So Sally, when I say 'sales', you can think of 'leads' instead."

"In either case," added Derek, "we're moving people from unaware to aware, from curious to interested, and from intrigued to invested."

"In fact," Ed reached over and popped up a new slide, "any of these events are worthy of our attention." *(Figure 9.6)*

Download

Registration

Subscription

Membership Submission

Contest Entry

Contact Request

Appointment Schedule Selection

Demonstration Request

Test Ride Request

Bike Configurator Usage

Price Calculator Usage

FIGURE 9.6

"I get your point. But let's just concentrate on sales here," Leo prompted.

"OK, here's an example," Ed replied. "Let's consider those people we talked about earlier, the people who had had reached Interest Stage 50 for the Silver Dollar bike. They've come to our site a few times, and some of them are close to hitting the 'Buy Now' button. We want to watch how long it takes them to make those purchases. Some online resellers have a 'one click' button that makes it possible to open one of their marketing messages, click through to the landing page, and make a purchase in under a minute. That's a very short sales cycle.

"Some of the elements that impact the sales process are largely outside of our control—for example, our customers will always need time to decide which color bike they like best. But we *can* manage the email offer and creative, and then identify which combinations result in the shortest sales cycle. This next report shows what I mean." *(Figure 9.7, p.95)*

"You can see here that Test Message #3 generated the most sales the fastest—but only during the first three weeks. After that, Test Message #1 overtook it significantly. From test campaigns like this one, in which we measure the overall value of each message and the length of their sales cycles, we'll ideally be able to combine the best elements to generate strong sales quickly."

FIGURE 9.7

"And that, in turn, will help us make better decisions about more expensive, offline promotions, assuming the audiences are similar enough across the different media." Derek added.

Ed stood up and walked to the projection screen. "The last few snapshots we've reviewed are good, but I'd really like to take you through the Silver Dollar test campaign from start to finish. So let's back up a step, and take a closer look."

"We started with a sample group of 10,000 people from our consumer database—that's 10% of the total. Here are some stats for three messages we've sent out." Ed pointed back to the screen.

	Message A	Message B	Message C
Sent to List 1	3,333	3,333	3.333
Bounced	80	0	50
Received	3,250	3,333	3,280
Opened	640	730	800
% Opened	19.7%	21.9%	24.4%

TABLE 9.1

"Message C is the clear winner so far. There's something about the time of day or the subject line that enticed more people to open it. But in the next set of data, you can see that Message B motivated more people to spread the word, but not enough to make a significant difference."

	Message A	Message B	Message C
Forwards	40	90	80
% Forwards	6.3%	12.0%	10.0%

TABLE 9.2

"Next, we shift focus to what these recipients did after they came to our site."

	Message A	Message B	Message C
Clickthroughs	240	250	260
% Clickthroughs	37.5%	33.3%	32.5%
Visit Duration *Minutes*	5	3	4
Visit Depth *Pages*	6	4	7
Avg. Interest Stage	40	50	50
Avg. Interest Points	28	65	50

TABLE 9.3

"Message C's lead is in question in this round. More people who received it clicked on a link to visit the site, but they didn't stay as long as the people who received Message A. They drilled deeper than the other messages, and did better or as well from the perspective of the Interest Stages, but Message B visitors scored a lot higher in the Interest Points category. In the end, though, what we really care about are the sales figures."

"Darn tootin'," Leo agreed.

"So, we look at sales not just by sheer quantity, but by how long it took from email to purchase, whether they came back to buy again, and the differences in purchase amount and profit.

"Here you can see that message C got more sales. Message C also made those sales faster, and pulled in more repeat sales for a grand total that more than doubled message B's success."

	Message A	Message B	Message C
Sales	60	40	70
Time-to-Sale *Days*	4	2	3
% Sales/Visits	25%	16%	27%
% Sales/Sends	1.8%	1.2%	2.1%
Repeat Sales	20	10	30
% Repeat Sales	33%	25%	43%
Total Sales/Message	80	50	100

TABLE 9.4

"So what was in C that got everybody reachin' for their wallets? Derek?"

"There were many factors at play here. In point of fact, messages A and C were identical. They were, however, sent out at different times of day and days of week. We're making an effort to be thorough in our research."

"So we needed a way to measure the actual value of each promotion," Ed continued. "Mark helped us with cost of goods sold, which we subtracted from the sale price of each bike. Then we subtracted a percentage we got from Penny for general and administration expenses, and finally we took out the cost of the email promotion itself.

"What's left is the profit we made on every sale, and the net profit of each test campaign."

	Message A	Message B	Message C
Total Sales/Message	80	50	100
Avg. Profit/Sale	$99	$79	$73
Gross Profit/Message	$7,920	$3,950	$7,300
Promotion Cost	$500	$500	$500
Net Profit/Message	$7,420	$3,450	$6,800

TABLE 9.5

Leo took it all in and replied, "So message C brought in more looky-loos and even made more sales, but it weren't the most profitable, so it's not the best promotion. Fair enough. But these are depressingly small numbers."

Derek raised a finger. "These are just the *test* runs, just as we would send test mailings to postal lists. We have an additional 90,000 people to contact, and we'll be doing more tests on email lists we plan to rent. Additionally, Ava will be ramping up the advertising."

"Don't I *know* it! If only I could tell if them TV ads were makin' money the way you can track your email, I'd be a lot happier about that ramping."

Ava had been steadfastly glued to her PDA during the majority of the meeting and Leo could no longer contain himself. "What has got you so hooked into that blasted machine?"

Ava looked at the group and reached for the data projector cable. She connected it to her PDA, and the screen resolved. (*Figure 9.8*)

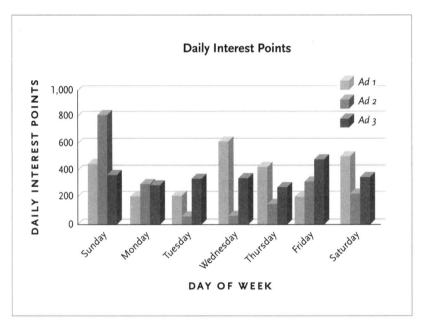

FIGURE 9.8

"Interest Points," read Leo "We see which ads generate the most interest. You got that on that little machine, do ya?"

Ava nodded. "Almost. We've been running three different test television ads in a few markets. This report shows the number of Interest Points generated by each ad on specific days." She paused.

All eyes were on Leo. "No foolin'."

"No foolin'. And here's another one, which shows the *cumulative* total Interest Points generated by each ad over the test campaign's run. You can see that Test Ads #1 and #3 are very similar overall, but there's some variance in the distribution of that interest over the test period." *(Figure 9.9)*

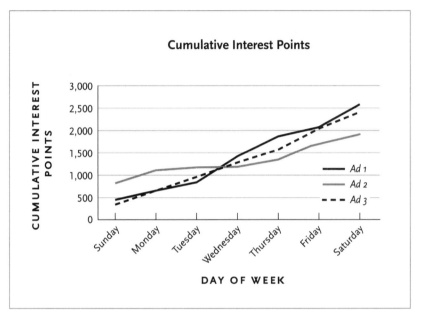

FIGURE 9.9

"So now we can track which ads on which days generate the most interest and," Ava said, calling up her last report, "we can see which television ads generated the most *sales*." *(Figure 9.10, p.100)*

"Well, I'll be." Leo's tone of voice revealed how impressed he was, but his face was a maelstrom of confusion. "OK, I get that we track a click from an email to the Web site. It's not that I doubt your word, Ava, it's just that I need to understand exactly what we're looking at here. How do you match a TV ad to a Web site visit?"

"It's not foolproof, but it's the most accurate method of measuring broadcast ads I've ever seen." With that, Ava tapped her PDA and one of the Silver Dollar test ads was up on the screen.

At the end of the ad, the voiceover said, "Visit AcmeBikeCorp Dot Com today and click on the bike helmet for your Silver Dollar discount. Limited time offer." The second ad

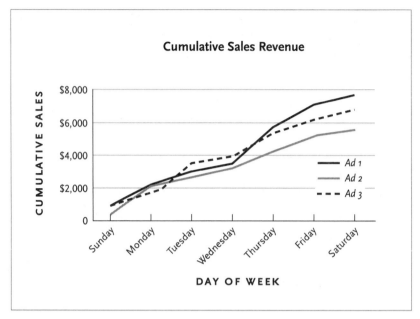

FIGURE 9.10

came up, and this time the voice over finished with, "...click on the bike wheel..." Ava let the machine play through the third and final ad.

"In each ad, we steer viewers to a different hidden link for a special Silver Dollar offer. If they click on that hidden link, we start tracking them for interest. This is how we're going to make you a lot happier about ramping up the advertising."

The room was quiet. They could see Leo's wheels turning.

"This is very good stuff and I'm pleased as can be, but I got one more problem and you gotta help me here. If you roll out these campaigns to the rest of our database, or to a whole bunch of other leads that ya' rent, we're gonna upset a whole lotta loyal retailers. They've been carryin' Acme bikes for years. Tell me, how are we're gonna make them happy?"

"Pay 'em," said Sally.

"Pay 'em?" Leo questioned.

"Give them a commission as if it were their sale," said Mark.

"Give *who* the commission?"

"At the time of sale, we display a list of nearby retailers and ask the buyer to choose," said Derek. "We already have a 'dealer locator' on our Web site, so it will be simple to come up with the correct list of dealers when a customer places an online order."

Leo smiled. "Pearl, I want you to start documentin' everything these Webified marketin' types are up to. If this works out like I think it will, we'll have a heck of a story to tell, but I want a one-year head start on everybody else. So we keep it under our hat for a spell. Understood?"

"Yes, sir," Pearl responded.

"And Tony, I want these youngins to earn their bonus this year, so you ride 'em hard and make sure they keep doin' what they're doin'."

"No, sir."

"And Ed..." Leo turned back to Tony. "Beg pardon?"

"Sorry, Dad. I won't be doing that."

"What are you sayin'?"

"I've done what I came to do, Dad. It's time to go."

"Done what? Go where? What are you *talkin'* about? You came here to help get this department turned around to keep it going in the right direction."

"The first part of that's right: I helped get the department turned around."

"But now you're gonna run it for me!"

"No, Dad, I'm not. See, I didn't do the turning around here. Mark did that. My job was to keep you off his back while he worked with the team. Mark's the right guy to take Victoria's place."

"But what about you? What about us?"

"I'm going to start my own company, a bicycle clothing line. My goal is to do well enough to buy you out in five years."

Leo was flummoxed. "*Buy* me out?! Five years?"

"Give or take. And I'm going to take Ed with me, to head up my marketing department, if he'll come."

Ed was surprised. Leo was shocked. "Take Ed?! No, no, no! I need him with here with me, to run the email and web tracking."

"He's done that already, Dad. He's got Derek up to speed on how the whole thing works, and Derek is the one with the creative experience. Besides, I'll lend Ed to you on a consulting basis every now and then. What do you say?"

"I say you're stealing my employees!"

"You've still got five years of running this place in you, don't you?"

"Well, of course I do. I got *ten* years! And it's going to take a hell of a lot of nerve and grit to buy *me* out! You're going to need all the help you can get, I can tell you that right now!"

"That's why I want you on my board of directors."

"On your what?"

"Board of directors, Dad. I'm going to need all the help I can get."

SUMMARY

- Gathering voluntary information about your list members not only enables you to personalize future campaigns, but also helps you improve the results of those campaigns on an ongoing basis.

- Closing the loop on your campaign entails processing many variables— revenue, time-to-sale, costs, etc.

- To track from "point of mail to point of sale" you'll need to invest in tools and people—the results of which will allow you to measure your goal achievement in monetary terms.

WORKSHEET

- Make a prioritized list of all of the demographic and psychographic information you'd like to gather about your prospects and customers. Remember to ask the most important questions first, in case your recipients balk at responding to subsequent queries.

- What process do you have in place to determine the cost of your campaigns and the value of the revenue they generate?

- Which messages in your recent email campaign were most profitable? Complete the following table with your results. If you don't have all of the data, what steps must you take to obtain it?

	Message A	Message B	Message C
Sent			
Received			
Opened			
Forwarded/Referred			
Clickthroughs			
Avg. Visit Duration			
Avg. Visit Depth			
Avg. Interest Points			
Avg. Interest Stage			
Sales ($)			
Avg. Time-to-Sale			
Repeat Sales ($)			
Total Sales ($)			
Avg. Profit ($)			
Gross Profit ($)			
Promotion Cost ($)			
Net Profit ($)			

CHAPTER 10 Conclusion

While Tony and Ed might spin off their new company, ride it to fame and fortune, and buy Leo out in three years instead of five, *you're* still on the hook for marketing miracles today. On a daily basis. You can do it, but it's going to take three things: goals, metrics, and teamwork.

GOALS

At every step of the way, you're going to have to know why you're stepping in any given direction. Socrates was onto something when he said, "The unexamined life is not worth living." Knowing what you want to accomplish is essential.

So ask "why" every time you're about to start another campaign, launch a new newsletter, or create an online contest. Once you know the reason—the goal—you can deconstruct that end into its constituent means. If you know why and how, you can start to identify specific milestones.

METRICS

What should you measure? Which events signify progress? Not in terms of project management, but in terms of getting a prospect to become a customer. Select specific Web pages, registration steps, or shopping cart behavior that serve as signposts that you're headed in the right direction. Then you can start collecting data and building the database.

TEAMWORK

Far beyond "playing well with others," the teamwork you need comes from developing very strong professional relationships, such that people from multiple disciplines within your organization can collaborate with their unique perspectives. Why is this important? Because they're going to bring ideas, creativity, and ownership to the table.

Establishing metrics that indicate progress are all well and good, and once you get them in place you can count yourself among the relatively few who do. An excellent start. But the *real* magic comes when you have a room full of high-IQ types who can look at the metrics reports and charts and graphs, and ask the really valuable, non-obvious questions. Continuous improvement is a fine thing. Breakthrough thinking is a whole other ballgame.

So bring your best goals, your most intricate metrics reports, and your smartest people together and breathe life into your marketing plans. Make the connections. Inspire each other. It's remarkably surprising just how much creativity a simple email can stimulate.

TOMORROW

As you identify your goals, define your metrics, and build your team, be sure that each step you take moves you in the right direction. It's great to go from walking to running to cycling to motoring, but you have to keep your bearings on a spot that's over the horizon at the moment.

In time, it will become obvious that email is the single best way to communicate with customers. It is individualized, immediate, and recordable. Email is much more analyzable than phone calls or store visits. Responses from your prospects and customers will one day find their way into your vast, yet-to-be-built database of customer opinion. The ability to sort and search through customer comments offers up a whole new realm of business opportunities.

The other over-the-horizon objective to keep in mind is marketing integration. Just as direct mail doesn't go out the door without a fulfillment plan; just as magazine ads are not placed without a call center to handle the calls; and just as banner ads are not served without a landing page in place, there quickly will come a time when successful marketing masters include an email component in all of their programs.

Your job is to have the vision. Your job is to pave the way. Your job is to keep everybody moving in the right direction to ensure that proper procedures and technologies are in place when the rest of the team wakes up to the power of email marketing done right.

Appendix:
Real, Unknown,
and Estimated Numbers

The art and science of measuring email delivery can be overwhelming. But it starts to make sense if you break it down into its various components: sends, deliveries, bounces, opens, and estimated opens.

Let's start with a real number: *sends.* Say you send out 2,783 messages to the people in your database meeting certain targeting criteria; your email server or marketing software will record that as the number of messages it sent. Likewise, if you use a list rental service, your list broker will confirm the total number of emails sent.

Sends are not, however, equivalent to *deliveries.* Since any list of email addresses will contain old data, the number of messages actually delivered will typically be a portion of your total sends. Addresses change or are taken out of service when people switch jobs, move from one email provider to another, or simply abandon their old accounts. Your list won't be up-to-date all the time, therefore, so some number of your messages will *bounce* or fail to be delivered for other reasons.

Bounces come in a few flavors. Hard bounces occur when an address no longer exists or, perhaps, never existed in the first place (for example, a misspelled name or domain). Email servers typically advise of a hard bounce with a "permanent delivery error" message. Soft bounces, in contrast, are the result of temporary or "transient" problems; full mailboxes or momentarily disabled mail servers are often the cause. Good email marketing software will retry these addresses at a later time, at which point the mail will probably go through correctly.

There's another reason why a message may be undeliverable—or, in this case, not be completely delivered: the anti-spam filter. Even though you may run a 100% confirmed opt-in list, some number of your recipients will be protected by anti-spam filters that block, reroute, or otherwise delete your mail. (*Figure 1, p.110*)

In scenarios like this, it's rare that you'll receive a bounce notice; in fact, you won't actually know if your mail was delivered or not. Anti-spam filters can be on individual recipients' computers, on departmental servers, at corporate gateways, or on ISPs' networks. These filters may block incoming mail for any number of reasons, based on: specific IP addresses or domains if they're

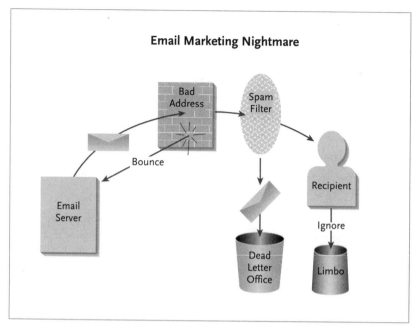

Email Marketing Nightmare

FIGURE 1

blacklisted or open relays; incorrectly formatted or apparently forged mail headers; or the content in the subject line or body of the message. To minimize this problem—and the "unknown" delivery factor—run a clean, opt-in list, test your messages against anti-spam filters, and maintain good relations with email providers and ISPs.

When your mail *is* delivered properly, how many *opens* do you really get? It's not possible to track opens for plain text, ASCII messages—unless you request an email "Return Receipt," and those drive people crazy. There is another way, but more on that later.

HTML mail is perfect for measuring opens. All you need to do is include a non-embedded graphic, usually a transparent image measuring one pixel by one pixel. When a mailing recipient opens an HTML message, it looks like a Web page. All of the embedded graphics have been delivered along with the email. A non-embedded graphic, however, won't be downloaded from your server until the message is opened by the recipient. It's small enough not to be noticed, but it's still recorded by the server that sent it. You can then see—either in your server logs or in the interface of your email marketing application—how many people opened your message and how often...almost.

Why aren't server logs exact calculators? Because some opens aren't "real" opens. For example, some email clients have a "preview" function that effectively opens each message on the user's behalf and downloads that non-embedded image. That means that your email marketing server records an open, but whether your recipient—or her mail client—saw the message is hard to know for sure.

Another component to consider is *estimated opens*. This metric allows you to gauge roughly how many people opened your plain text messages, by applying the HTML message open rate to your entire list of mailing recipients.

On a list of 1,000 people, for example, let's say that 600 have HTML-enabled mail clients and the balance read text-only. If you sent a mailing and measured a 30% open rate—of the HTML-enabled folks—the estimated open figure would be 300: 180 HTML-readers (30% of 600) and 120 text-readers (30% of 400). (*Figure 2*)

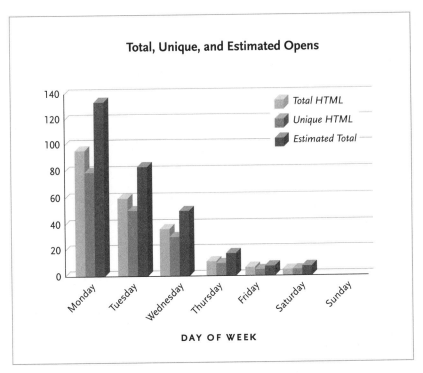

FIGURE 2

Here's a final thought and important reminder: it's easy to get caught up in your stats, but the absolute numbers themselves aren't too critical. Deliveries, bounces, and opens all have an unknown element to them, but what ultimately matters are changes in delivery, bounce, and open *rates* from one mailing to the next. Keep an eye out, then, for surprising blips or interesting long-term trends.

Index

NOTES

NOTES

NOTES

NOTES

NOTES

NOTES

NOTES

NOTES

NOTES

NOTES

NOTES

NOTES